T0129859

UNWINDING THE DIVINE MASCULINE

DISCOVERING THE SECRETS TO DIVINE UNION AND SACRED LOVE

VELVA DAWN SILVER

BALBOA.PRESS
A DIVISION OF HAY HOUSE

Balboa Press books may be ordered through booksellers or by contacting:

Balboa Press
A Division of Hay House
1663 Liberty Drive
Bloomington, IN 47403
www.balboapress.com
844-682-1282

www.velvadawn.com

Print information available on the last page.

ISBN: 979-8-7652-3263-7 (sc)
ISBN: 979-8-7652-3262-0 (hc)
ISBN: 979-8-7652-3261-3 (e)

Library of Congress Control Number: 2022914466

Balboa Press rev. date: 09/01/2022

To all of the men who are struggling to awaken, this
book is dedicated to your inner journey.
I see your need to want to change, but the fear of knowing how
and feeling safe shines underneath the old coats of masculine
armor. I dedicate this book to my dad, Neil David Silver,
for showing me courage, unconditional love, compassion,
and nurturing and to my granddad, David Strachan Silver,
for giving me the deep masculine roots of trust.

CONTENTS

INTRODUCTION

A Journey into the Awakening Masculine Heart

The masculine stereotype has shifted over the years. I grew up in a rural farming community, and in this area, men worked hard from dawn to dusk. My granddad and dad were mixed grain and cattle farmers. These two men were my role models, introducing the masculine energy into my life. I have very fond memories of Granddad Dave Silver. I would sit for hours as he would share stories of coming over to Canada from Scotland with his family as a young boy. He was a hardworking man with an open heart. I remember when one of my uncles was dying from AIDS back in 1988, Granddad had a huge stack of photocopied papers on his side table by his armchair in the living room. I asked him what all those papers were for. He replied, "Well, I need to educate myself on what exactly this disease is that is killing my son."

I was so proud to know that he wasn't too proud to educate himself on whatever he needed to.

My fondest memories of my granddad were walking out to the garage where he would sit at his lath and create beautiful clocks from many different types of wood. I would join him out there, he would show me what he was making, and then he would ask me about my life. When I was in high school, I would tell him about my troubles with boys and relationships. He would listen and sometimes give me advice but mostly just listen and let me cry sometimes.

On Friday nights, I would walk over to my grandparents' house, which was only a few steps away from the house that I was raised in on the family farm. I would knock on the door and walk up into the family room where my grandparents were usually watching a hockey game. As soon as I would sit down, they would shut off the television. I would always say to Granddad, "You don't have to shut off the television," and he would say, "Yes, I do as nothing is more important than talking to those who mean something to you."

Side note: Remember, personal connection is something that your kids will remember down the road. It's been thirty-one years and I still remember the impact of being present in my grandparents' connection. They will remember when you make time for them and are present.

We would talk for hours, sometimes surface but mostly deep, talking about life and why things were the way they were from each of our perspectives. My granddad would go deep in conversation with me. This is where I learned that it was safe to talk deeply about my feelings and to understand why family dynamics were the way they were sometimes. I have always felt comfortable talking to men deeply, and this stems from the sacred relationship with my granddad.

When James, my first husband, asked me to marry him, my granddad was over the moon because he was delighted that I would be marrying a cattle rancher whose grandfather also liked a glass of good scotch. I wanted to keep my maiden surname and then add on my husband-to-be's surname. My granddad said to me, "Why would you do this?"

I said, "Because don't you think that Silver is a good name?"

He answered with a smirk, "Well, yes, I can't disagree with you on that one."

I said, "Granddad, my surname is important to me, and I also want my future kids to have the name Silver as part of their middle names to remember both sides of the families."

In the end, I also mentioned to Granddad that it was the "thing" to do now. He laughed and said, "Okay, I understand."

He was always willing to listen to the newest idea and then sit with it before he came to his own opinion. I loved this about him. I feel so grateful to have had such loving grandparents live so close to me growing up.

I remember my grandma calling me one day when I was about thirty years old, telling me that Granddad had some heart troubles and was in the CCU at the Red Deer Hospital. I immediately got in the car and drove to see him. When I was able to see him, the first words from his mouth were "So this is what I had to do to get a pretty girl like you to come and see her granddad."

He always made me smile, no matter what was going on his world.

This was the beginning of those deep masculine roots for me, to feel safe sharing deeply with the masculine in my life; the beginning of the masculine heart connection.

Trust that those beginning relationships with the opposite sex have a profound effect on future relationships with those around us. Don't take those moments for granted as they foster health.

My dad, Neil Silver, is a hardworking family man. He dedicated many hours to his family, his community, and his work.

He has a gentle heart. I remember being about ten years old and I was having pain in my chest area. I was very fearful that I was having a heart attack. I finally worked up the courage to share with my mom that I was having this chest pain, and she laughed at me and said, "Honey, I promise you that you aren't having a heart attack."

The pain didn't stop, and I didn't want to tell her again, so I waited until my dad came inside from his farm work. He sat on the couch beside me and said, "What is going on with your heart?"

I said, "I feel like I am having a heart attack."

He calmly told me that at my age, this was highly unlikely. I trusted him, and this reassurance put me at ease. Looking back, I now understand that it was most likely anxiety from hormones of being a preteen and being highly empathic.

My mom was the disciplinarian when I was growing up. I remember wanting to rebel and stay out past my curfew. So one night I was determined to do just that! What happened was I fell asleep at my boyfriend's house and woke up at 5:00 a.m. I was not so brave at this time to be driving home and facing my mother. When I tried to sneak in at 5:30 a.m., I was met by my dad putting his chore clothes on to go outside and check the cows that were calving. He said to me, "Isn't it a little late to be coming home?"

I said, "I know, I fell asleep."

He didn't give me a hard time; he just quietly but firmly let me know that I shouldn't disrespect my curfew again.

He has a gentle yet firm way of letting you know when you had done something out of respect and integrity. I appreciate this about my dad to this day. He has been my rock, supporting me through the unwinding of my twenty-one-year marriage through divorce. There is nothing like a solid masculine energy to bounce off ideas or a shoulder to cry on.

The lineage of the deep roots of communication came from my granddad Dave, flowing down into my dad Neil. We must always remember to do the thing that feels best in our hearts and to have compassion, patience, and unconditional love for others as it does feed the lineage.

The old patriarchal ways of connection, creation, and being are unwinding thread by thread one soul at a time. As the light enters each man, they discover the inner awareness that the divine feminine has always known. The women will begin to awaken the new divine masculine within, and collectively, we will cocreate a new heart based on foundational life together. The old ways of segregating for control and power will no longer serve the highest greater collective and won't be a vibrational match for many.

As we shed the layers of this old segregation during the COVID-19 pandemic, we no longer have the choice to live in an unconscious world. The gift will be the shift in priorities connected to the heart and passion. Old ways of exploiting energy will be shed into the earth with no vibrational match in the DNA of the people.

CHAPTER 1

The Unwinding

Name: James
Occupation: Rancher
Age: 26
Height: 6'0"

Unwinding twenty-one years of marriage isn't an easy thing to do, nor is it for the faint of heart. Sometimes it is necessary for one's own internal growth.

James was my world for twenty-one-plus years. We met in the local bar to hear a mutual friend sing live music. I had no intention of dating again ever. I was dating a man from the area where I was working at the local hospital in medical records. I knew that I wasn't his forever girl, but what I didn't realize was that he was "dating" another girl at the same time as he was dating me. He came to me one day after a casual twelve-month relationship and told me that this would be the last time that we could see each other because he was getting married to a woman who was pregnant with his child. Boom! That rocked my heart. From that moment, I decided that I wasn't dating anyone and that I would get myself a puppy as a companion. No more broken heart for this girl.

Then on a cold night in January 1995, I decided to go to a local neighboring bar with my softball team to watch a fellow teammate sing.

A mutual friend came over to me and said, "There is a man standing by the pole with a cowboy hat on that is interested in you."

I sat there for a minute trying to be nonchalant and looked over my shoulder to see if I would be interested. I finally had enough courage to walk to the washroom and get a good look, up and down, at him. I stopped on the way back and introduced myself to him. This man would be the first adult love of my life and the father to my three beautiful daughters.

His name was James. He told me that he would call me on Monday, and he did just that. He followed through and was accountable to his actions. He asked me to go to supper at the closest thing to a five-star restaurant that our local town had. I was nervous as you can imagine. Going on any first date is nerve-racking, and having to eat a meal in front of a man I wanted to impress gave me butterflies.

I worked in the local hospital, so I asked a lot of coworkers if they knew of him and/or his family. The response was positive, so I was excited to go. As we entered the restaurant, I saw a large table of coworkers from the hospital having a supper meeting. My heart began to race because I realized that many of them would be gently watching to see how my date was going. I was the single young girl working at a small hospital, so they were always trying to match me up with the most recent doctor, anesthesiologist, or pharmacist!

He was a gentleman right from the get-go. He opened the door of his truck for me and the door to the restaurant. He was an old-fashioned man at heart. He treated me just how my granddad and dad had shown me a girl was to be treated by a man. The supper went well that night, and then he came back to my house for a bit.

I had a purebred Cocker Spaniel named Molly. When James sat down on my couch, Molly ran over to him and sat down on his lap and peed on him. I was mortified! He laughed and said, "Well, I think that she likes me and/or is marking her territory."

I ran into my kitchen to grab a tea towel while giggling to myself, thinking this might be the last date! He kissed me as he left that evening. I genuinely knew that there was something different about James. He was different from the rest of the men I had dated—in a good way.

We continued to see each other for many months, getting to know each other on a deeper level. He would call me at the hospital during my lunch break, and we would talk for at least thirty minutes. I remember calling him at his parents' house as that is where he went for lunch. Sometimes, if his dad answered the phone, I couldn't tell if it was James or his dad, so I would ask a few questions until I had clarity on which man I was speaking to.

One day there were a dozen red roses on my desk at work when I came back from my break. Joan, one of my coworkers, was grinning from ear to ear, and she said, "I think that someone sent you some flowers!"

I looked at the card, and it said, "Love, James."

I reread the card a few times to make sure what I was seeing was the word *love*. Then I pondered that thought for quite some time. I thought, *How could he love me so soon?*

James was very genuine in all he said and did. He showed up when he said he would, and I liked the fact that he too was from an agricultural background. When he asked what type of cattle my dad ran, I could easily answer black Maine-Angus cross. He laughed and said that he was happily surprised that I could answer that question. I am a woman with many facets. I can put on a pair of Carhartt overalls and sort cattle or slide into a pair of high heels with a silk dress to go out! I am truly grateful for my upbringing with rural roots, which gifts me the stability in many areas of life.

I knew that I was beginning to fall in love with James too. We had a lot of similarities that connected our hearts right from the beginning. I remember driving home from working at the hospital one afternoon. His mom was driving in front of me and pulled her car over on the side of the road and invited me to pull over too. I was thinking to myself, *Oh, she's not happy that I am staying overnight with her son on the ranch.*

Well, it was exactly the opposite of that. She very firmly told me how much she liked me and that she knew I was spending a lot of time with her son on the ranch and that maybe I should move in with him to save money on gas and that she had no problem with us living together before we were engaged. Wow! I was happily surprised that she was so forthright with me but appreciated her bold, loving gesture. This was just the beginning of a deep friendship with her, which I will be forever grateful for.

Finally, we started talking about engagement rings months down the road. I knew I had always wanted a heart-shaped diamond since I was a little girl. We drove into the city and went to a diamond store to do some research. We sat down with the salesperson and shared what we were looking for and how much he was willing to spend. I opted out to hear that part of the conversation as the value wasn't important to me. I was excited that we were moving to the next level in our relationship. This one felt different. I could feel this deep knowing inside of me that we would be together for a long time.

I waited in his truck as he closed the conversation with the salesman. He told me that he had to sell a bull before he could order the ring. I smiled and told him that I could wait for that to happen. Then on August 24, 1995, James asked me to make my special homemade pizza for supper and to pick up a bottle of white zinfandel wine as I made my way back to the ranch after work that day. I had a feeling that something was up but couldn't figure out if he had ordered the engagement ring or not.

It was baling season on the ranch, and he was spending long hours baling hay before the rain hit. I understood this, being raised on a mixed cattle and grain farm my whole life. I picked up the supplies and made my way back to the ranch where I began to make the homemade pizza crust in the bread machine. I loved to make Hawaiian pizza from scratch. I lit a few candles and poured some wine, setting the ambiance for a romantic evening.

James came in and showered, and I prepared the meal. I had butterflies in my stomach as I had a feeling that he may propose to me that night. We sipped our wine while eating pizza and talking about the day. Then all of a sudden, he got down on one knee by my chair at the kitchen table and asked me to marry him. I said, "Yes! I will marry you."

My intuition was right! It was a magical night and the beginning of building a lifetime together.

Six months after meeting, we were engaged. James proposed to me on his parents' wedding anniversary, which I thought was kind of a cool thing to weave the energy together down the lineage of family. He gave me a gold band with a heart-shaped diamond and two baguette diamonds on either side of the heart-shaped solitaire. I loved it! We phoned our sets of parents and told them that we were engaged. We had no cell phones back then. It was the old-fashioned corded telephone that was used in sharing our happy news. The time when we knew the phone numbers of those around us.

Our families were very happy about our engagement. Even our grandparents were happy about it as we had a lot of similarities in our upbringing and our family values. The blending of our two families paired well, you could say.

Fast-forward to January 20, 1996, at 2:30 p.m., we were married in the same church that my parents were married in thirty years previously. We were surrounded by friends and family to the tune of more than one hundred people. We had a lot of similar interests, so our families blended very well from the beginning. My dad and James became good friends as I did with James's mom Mary.

We had our first daughter born in late May 1997, followed by our second daughter three years later also in late May 2000, and then our third daughter in July 2003. James's grandfather would always tease us, saying that we needed to try to have a boy to run the family's ranch. We smiled and said, "We are happy with three healthy girls and that they are quite capable of doing anything that a boy can do."

As we moved through the years of our marriage, we raised the girls, started the local 4-H Beef Club together, grew our own careers, and did the best that we knew how. As many of you know, having a baby and starting a family doesn't come with an instruction manual. The first years of marriage can be blissful yet incredibly challenging at times. I was raised on a cattle and grain farm, so I was familiar with the long hours of working outdoors, moving cattle, baling hay, the numerous brandings attended, and then there is calving season. The night shifts, cold days, and short tempers took their toll on our relationship.

As our girls grew, we began to grow apart and then back together. Our marriage was evolving as we were growing. We had very similar values with our upbringing and rural roots. I began to feel that something was missing deep within my soul. When I was pregnant and gave birth to our daughters, I soon began to question life after death. I now felt the responsibility that I am sure our own parents recognized years previous. I had brought these souls into the world and now have experienced love in a way that I have never felt before. Many times the feeling would give me anxiety from the overwhelming magnitude of this role, being a mother to three beautiful daughters.

As we moved through our years parenting our three girls, I began unraveling my spiritual awakening. I began to take many courses to open my intuitive abilities and dabble in the metaphysical realm. As you can imagine, being married to a cattle rancher and beginning this career, I began to stir the awakenings of those around me. I knew that many of them were thinking, "What is this woman doing with all her essential oils, and what are 'chakras'?"

I found a deep sense of inner peace connecting internally to myself and began to see life through a whole new spectrum. I felt a wholeness opening up inside of myself. I began to feel secure in what I had always known about life and was ready to begin weaving this insight into my roles as a wife and mother and in my career, friendships, and community.

This new connection was truly the beginning of the end for our marriage, I believe. I outgrew the role of what James had known me for at the altar the day that we exchanged our wedding vows. He was supportive of my new ventures and supporting me in renovating his grandparents' old house into a retreat center for my new business. I quit my job in health care to go back to school to become a natural health practitioner for two years. I then wrote my first book *Ancient Secrets of the Goddesses* and created The Goddess Healing Matrix System. This system is a four-level program designed to assist people who are ready to release old traumas, expand their intuition, increase their self-confidence and to begin looking within for all wisdom through the lens of the divine feminine.

As we moved through growing our respective careers, we began to grow apart even more. His focus was on cattle and agriculture, and mine was on the empowerment of women through the archetypes of the goddess. We built a home in Hawaii together as I felt strongly called to be closer to the elements of the ocean and island energy. We would spend time together there as a family for seasonal holidays.

One summer I took all three girls and my dog to Hawaii. I asked

James to come for a few weeks to enjoy some down time together as a family. He would always say that the weight of the responsibility of the ranch came first and that he couldn't spare that much time. He came for a week at the beginning and a week at the end of that particular summer. This is where the true growth for me occurred. I began to expand my self-confidence being a mom to three girls, exploring the island, and learning new activities, such as surfing, swimming in the ocean, getting PADI certified, and running a household in an exotic climate, a.k.a. learning how to live where hurricanes, earthquakes, active volcanoes, and how to be free from getting bitten from scorpions and centipedes that existed in this world. My awakening from the prairie to the ocean world quickly began.

I remember coming home from spending three months in Hawaii with the girls. I could feel the disconnection within our marriage. I felt a vast inner growth and strength from being on my own, which I hadn't experienced since before we were married. No matter how much you try to avoid being codependent in a marriage, it can just happen as I felt it did for me. This summer was a wake-up call for me. I could feel the separation between James and I ignited from my own inner growth. I talked openly about how I felt to him and was holding space that he would join me in this new expanded perception of life outside of what we had known for the last seventeen years of our marriage.

He seemed open to seeing these new perceptions with me at times, but truly, I feel that our time together was complete. My inner knowing was very strong once again. I feel that we had been fighting the obvious for a few years now. I had outgrown the path of being a rancher's wife with a part-time occupation. I needed something more for myself. That summer gave me the tools that I needed to have the confidence and trust in following my own path and gaining clarity on who I was now and what I needed as my own woman. I began to realize that I left parts of myself along the journey of being married to a rancher and raising three girls, which naturally can happen. I was afraid to show people who I truly was for fear of judgment within a small community.

Fast-forward to February 2016, I was on the phone with my event coordinator Cody, and we were discussing the annual Shine . . . Ignite Your Inner Goddess event. I began to have pain in my chest, which was moving down my left arm and up to my left jaw. Now being previously in the medical field for over fifteen years, I knew that these were strong symptoms of a heart attack. I asked Cody if it was the left side that was the side for pain of a heart attack, and she said, "Yes."

She asked me if I was having a heart attack, and I said, "Yes, I was pretty sure that I was."

She offered to come be with me, but she lived over forty minutes away, so I told her that I would call 911.

James and I had had a serious discussion earlier that morning regarding our marriage and what the next step was going to be for our relationship. He left the house angry with me and said that he had to go into town for an appointment. So when this chest pain began, I called him several times to ask him to come back and help me. He never returned my phone call or my text message. He later told me that he left his cell phone in the vehicle for his appointment, so he had no idea that I needed help. I began to look outside our kitchen window in the bale yard for my father-in-law who helps with chores each morning to see if he could help me. I couldn't see him anywhere out feeding cows like his normal morning routine. I knew that I was alone on the ranch, and then suddenly, it dawned on me that I might die alone.

I called my good friend Kathy as I knew that she was in a town close by for an appointment. She answered the phone immediately and asked, "Are you okay?"

I urgently replied, "No, I am pretty sure that I am having a heart attack!"

She said, "Oh my! I will be right there!"

As I was waiting for her, I began to sweat profusely, and I knew that I had to call 911. I was so stubborn that I refused to call 911 first as I was in denial that I was a forty-four-year-old woman and that I could be having a heart attack. I was on a juicing regime, exercised regularly, and cleared my chakras, so how in the hell could I be having a heart attack? I decided to call 811 first. The nurse urgently said to me, "Ma'am, you are having a heart attack, so I need you call 911 now, please!"

I told her that my friend could drive me to the nearest hospital or that I could drive myself. She said, "No, ma'am, you need medical attention, stat, and the paramedics can administer life-saving drugs if you need them!"

So I decided that I needed to put on some clean underwear first as my mom had always told me to have clean underwear on in case I needed to go to the hospital. Well, here was that time that she was talking about! Who makes up this stuff anyhow? As I was bent over to put on my clean underwear, I was sweating even more profusely now and was truly scared that I might die alone, naked, with no underwear on! It became real that I might die in my home and that my body had a mind of its own. I called 911, and the responder went through a list of questions, and she said she had dispatched an ambulance from the local hospital and that the local fire department was also dispatched. I told her that I didn't want the local fire department dispatched as I knew all the volunteers and that I didn't want them to know what was going on with my health. She told me that she had to dispatch them in case they could be there faster than the ambulance. She asked me if I had any aspirin in my medicine cabinet, and I said, "Yes, I bought the aspirin for my parents or in-laws in case they had a heart attack," that it wasn't for me.

She told me to take two aspirins immediately and put them under my tongue. I did so in much shock and disbelief.

My friend Kathy arrived through the back door of the garage. By then, I was sitting on the couch with my trusty dog Laila, pondering the fact that I might be dying. She calmly walked through the door and said, "How are you doing, my friend?"

I said, "I am scared."

Laila was sitting very close to me as I feel as though she could feel the stress that my body was in. Kathy calmly asked me if I had called 911 and if the ambulance was on its way, and I said, "Yes, they were."

She helped me gather a few things to put into my purse to take in the ambulance. She then sat by me on the couch, helping me remain as calm as one can be while having a heart attack. The local fire department arrived first by only a couple of minutes. They asked me a few questions about my symptoms. The EMS came through the front door next, assessing my condition as I sat on the couch. They began to administer nitroglycerin spray to help reduce the pain in my chest. Then they asked me to get on the gurney as they wanted to load me into the ambulance to be en route to the local hospital, which I previously worked at. Now being an Aries astrologically, I tend to be stubborn! Ram tough is one of the qualities of an Aries. So I didn't want to lie on the gurney and have them carry me down the steps of the front of the house, so I walked to the ambulance in my slippers and then laid down on the gurney.

My friend Kathy drove behind the ambulance. She took my phone with her so she could let my husband know that what was going on. I was worried that my father-in-law would see the ambulance leaving the ranch and that he would worry about what was going on. I asked Kathy to text my husband to let him know that I was en route to the local hospital with a query heart attack. She also called my stepmother-in-law and told her what was happening in case anyone saw the flashing lights of the ambulance leaving the dirt roads of the ranch.

I was grateful that my girls were all in school that day, so they didn't have to experience seeing me in this situation. Upon arriving at the local rural hospital, the emergency room doctor took some blood and said that he would be back with the results soon. I was talking with Kathy about what this was going on inside my chest and truly was in shock during this time. Soon the doctor came in, and he said, "Your blood tests show that you have an increase in troponin, which tells me that your heart muscle is being damaged."

He told me that I would be going to a city hospital immediately to be seen by a cardiologist. He also informed me that I needed to call a family member and inform them of my condition. Now I knew that this was serious! I called my dad and told him that they thought that was I was having a cardiac event and that I was being transported to a city hospital, stat. His response still brings tears to my eyes. He said, "Kiddo, you are way too young to be having a heart attack."

He asked me to keep him informed of what was happening to me and to have Kathy keep him informed through it all.

As they were loading me in the ambulance bay into a second ambulance to go into the city hospital, my husband called my cell phone. He said, "Dad just told me that you were having a heart attack?"

I answered him with "Yes, I am having a heart attack, and I am being transferred to a city hospital as we speak."

He said that he would drive in and meet me at the hospital. My eldest daughter was already living in the city, so she was waiting at the hospital when I arrived via ambulance. The emergency room beds were all full, so I had to wait in the hallways with one of the paramedics until a room became available. They had to keep administering the nitro spray under my tongue and checking my vitals frequently. The emergency room doctor began assessing me and concurred with the diagnosis that I was having a cardiac event and that I would have to be admitted to the cardiac coronary care unit as soon as a bed became available. My husband came down the hallway where I was lying on the gurney waiting for a bed, and I could hear him telling the doctor that I was going to be fine. The doctor said, "Sir, your wife is having a cardiac event," that this was serious.

I am sure he was in as much shock as I was. I could see the tears in my eldest daughter's eyes as she was watching the process. I was trying to be strong for her in holding my own tears back. Truth be told, I was damn scared. I had never experienced chest pain like that before, and being along with the pain had already ignited the PTSD.

I spent the night in a room in the emergency room department. It was a long night of multiple tests and ECG leads attached to my chest. I was so scared. James went home to be with our girls, and my good friend Kellie stayed with me through the night, sleeping in a chair beside me. I was so grateful for her staying with me because I didn't want to be alone in case I did die that night. I didn't sleep at all as I lay there wondering why this was happening to me. Why didn't my husband answer his phone when I called him? This must be a clear sign from the universe that our marriage was over.

Early the next morning, there was space for me to be admitted in the cardiac intensive care/coronary care unit in the hospital. I remember the EMTs came to move me up to the cardiac intensive care/coronary care unit. As I waited near the closed glass doors of the CCU no. 3 room, where I was going to spend the next five days of my life, I looked around and saw through the glass doors people who were struggling to remain alive. It hit me! I was seriously this ill.

As they wheeled my gurney into the room, they began to hook up the sixteen leads to my chest. I could see that the toilet was right next to my bed; no separate bathroom. This was serious business. I was happy to have my own private room but seriously not under these circumstances. The nurse began to write my differential diagnoses on the white board in my room. There were five of them. I read each of them, and I truly didn't want to dig too deep into what they were. My good friend, who is also in the medical field, came by for a quick visit, and she looked at the diagnoses and said to me, "You know these are all quite serious diagnoses."

I replied, "I know," but I was in too much shock to truly think much past the pounding pain in my head from the nitro patch.

As I lay in the bed, I truly began pondering my life up until this point. Was I happy? Did I accomplish all that I had wanted to? Would my girls be okay if I died? Was my marriage over? Would I be healthy again? Why didn't my intuitive friends tell me that this was going to happen? How could my body betray me? Would I live a normal life again?

My husband brought my girls in to visit me after they were done with school that day. When you are admitted into cardiac intensive care/coronary care unit, you can only enter if you aren't sick. I could see the worry in the girls' eyes as they saw all the leads attached to my body and the monitors connected to show my vitals. My middle daughter had my husband buy me a stuffed bunny rabbit toy from the gift store as she said it would remind me of petting my dog Laila, and she hoped that it would bring me comfort since she didn't think that she could sneak her into the hospital. Seeing my three daughters brought me so much comfort after a long two days of fear and pain.

James came in one day and let out a big sigh. I said to him, "You don't need to come and visit me if you don't want to be here."

I am a big believer that the energy you bring into a room affects the people in the room. I needed true support during this time as I was scared to my very core. My dad couldn't come visit me as he was sick, and they won't allow anyone who is sick into the cardiac intensive care/coronary care unit. He sent his sister, my aunt Gerry, to come visit me. She walked through the closed curtains in my glass cubicle and said, "Your dad sent me to make sure that you are okay as he is sick and is very worried about you."

I could see the concern on her face also. At this point, I was numb to the seriousness of my health as I was inside my own head trying to work through my own queries and scenarios. I had no energy for trying to connect with many outside of that tiny room. I just had no energy left.

The nitro patch gave me one of the worst headaches that I have ever experienced. I wanted to make the pain go away so badly. My daughters came in that day with my husband, and I told him that it wasn't a good day for me to be around anyone as I was deeply struggling. The sleepless nights of nurses' checks and monitors going off were taking its toll on my mental health. I truly began pondering my life, my marriage, which was falling apart already, and my purpose.

One morning the nurse came in with a consent form for an angiogram to further diagnose my heart. They told me that it would be performed at another city hospital and that I would need to go via ambulance that morning. I looked at my husband and asked if he would be able to come and he said that he was going to the girls' school for an awards ceremony. There it was! This was the clarity that I had been asking for from the universe. Our marriage was so severed at this point that there was no turning back. I was extremely scared for this test, and James had made a choice to now show up at my side on this critical moment yet again. Clarity was vivid now.

All my tests were clear during that stay in the cardiac intensive care/coronary care unit, and I was discharged without a firm diagnosis of what caused the troponin levels to increase. I did consult with an intuitive friend who told me that I was slowly dying because of the lack of joy and love in my heart. I knew that this was truth as I had felt the energetic pain within my heart for many years already.

I allowed myself time to recover from this experience. I struggled with sleeping alone in fear of dying alone for months after being discharged. I even asked my husband to sleep on the couch near my bedroom so that I felt safe in case my heart gave out on me again. He did for a bit, and then I had my youngest daughter sleep with me. I realize now that I suffered from PTSD for a long time after this incident.

I faxed in a retainer for my lawyer a few months previous to this to begin the process of our separation, and now I had affirmation, through my illness, of the physical finality of our connection. I knew that I would want my husband to stay with me through each moment of a critical illness. I know that I am strong, but in this scenario, I would choose to be supported by my spouse.

Four months later, during a checkup with my cardiologist, they found a blood clot in my right popliteal vein. Later, after having a specialized VQ lung scan, they confirmed two pulmonary emboli in the right lower lobe of my lungs. I was put on anticoagulants for a few months and was referred to a respiratory specialist to follow up. To this day, I see my cardiologist annually for a thorough checkup and further testing. I am in good hands with this cardiologist.

This experience with my health forever changed the way I live my life and view life. My new motto is #yolo. As James and I began to unwind our twenty-one-year marriage, it took its toll on my mental health, with my physical health not far behind. As scared as I was to unwind this marriage, I knew once again that I had to take this next step to heal and find my own happiness.

I knew that staying together because we had children wasn't healthy for anyone, and I prayed that the process wouldn't harm any of us too badly along the way. I knew that I would die if I stayed in this marriage as it had fulfilled its role in my life.

We hired lawyers and began the process of working through our biggest fears. It was a messy process of fear, anger, unknowing, and loss of what we had known for so many years. The death of a marriage can be complicated through the highest of intentions.

We had many moments in the mediation room where our emotions got the best of us. I had an ah-ha moment during one of the grueling three to four mediation sessions with three lawyers in the room. Here we are with these strangers who don't even know us and they are prepping us on how to tear apart the very sacred union of our family! I was shocked and sickened that our twenty-one-year marriage had to end like this. I called James and asked him if we could talk and sort this out between the two of us just like we had begun. He agreed. We came to a mutual decision for how the ending looked for each of us. We walked into mediation that morning and told our lawyers what we wanted that to look like, and it was time to write the separation agreement. You see, when you are in the process of divorce, your emotions can lead the way, and it's hard to use your business brain.

We finished the process, and then we each began our own journeys to heal. I don't even remember those months during the process. It was like a blur. I do remember lying in the fetal position on the heated kitchen tile floor one time, wanting my life to end, as the pain within my heart was too much. I worried constantly through the process that I would die from this deep pain.

At this current moment, my two eldest girls have chosen to distance themselves from me as their mother. This has been the greatest loss in the unraveling of my marriage to James. Divorce is hard enough, but to lose your relationship as a mom, your community, and your infrastructure of family has hit me hard. I struggled seeing my general doctor weekly and my counselor. I chose not to go on antidepressants as I wanted to feel the pain of what I was going through versus numbing; my personal belief for myself. I did have a moment of wanting to give up, and I was on my way to the ranch to drive my car off a bridge to end all the pain.

My girlfriend Fawna called me, and we talked through the situation, diffusing the urge to end my pain. She was very good at guiding me back to what my long-term focus was and that this too shall pass. I have to say that I have an amazing group of strong friends that supported me through those messy times.

Not too long ago, I went to see my counselor, and she said to me, "Girl, I didn't think that you were going to make it, but you did, and I am so proud of you!"

That brought tears to my eyes because I had many moments that I didn't want to make it either! Through time, medical support, counseling, and energy healing, my grieving process is almost full circle, moving into acceptance.

I know that James and I had fulfilled our roles in each other's lives in a martial relationship. Our marriage helped me unwind the masculine programming that was embedded throughout my life. I knew that I had to take the next step upon my journey solo, which was necessary. As hard as it was to initiate the process of divorce, my heart showed me clearly the way that I needed to go.

Do I believe that everyone who begins to awaken on his or her spiritual journey needs to get divorced? Absolutely not. Each journey of awakening is unique to each person. Would I go back and change the process? Yes, some things I would have put more thought into my choices versus being fueled by sheer emotion.

I will always be grateful for that shy man named James who asked me on a date on January 20, 1995. Our lives together had come full circle, and it was time to grow my wings and fly solo.

"The trail winds onward through the hills

From here to prairies end;

Will our journey ever last?

As long as you're my love, my friend."

This was a poem that was on our wedding invitation. It was the one of the circles in my flower of life journey, and so it is.

CHAPTER 2

The Rebound

Name: Luke
Age: 48
Occupation: Heavy-equipment operator
Height: 6'1"

Signs from the divine or not!

When red flags are waving at you and you live in denial!

Unhealed childhood wounds end up being combined with wounds in future relationships unless they are addressed previously. This was my first attempt at online dating. I felt ready to begin connecting with the dating world again. It had been more than twenty-three years since I had been on a date! I didn't even know where to begin. There were so many dating apps to choose from, which one was better and how did they work.

I decided to go with the one I had heard of the most. My first step was to put on something that I felt good wearing, curl my hair, and put on makeup. Then I went outside and stood in front of the green trees and took some selfies. I felt so awkward. I remember that the sun was shining down on my face, and I thought to myself, *Well this would be good lighting to use.*

This is my first memory of being single and awkwardly learning what a selfie was all about.

I decided to create a profile on this dating app. There were so many questions to answer, and I had to write a profile paragraph about myself and what I was looking for. Really? First off, I was already struggling, feeling like a failure from my twenty-one-year marriage. Why would any man want to date a forty-five-year-old mother of three almost adult daughters?

My self-esteem was already in the bucket, being rejected by my husband of twenty-one years. I certainly didn't feel like the sexual being that I was when I was dating in my twenties. I began counseling before we entered into the decision to divorce, and I would recommend this to anyone who is considering leaving his or her intimate relationship. The one key point that my counselor said to me was, "Dawn, make sure that you have turned over every stone before you decide to leave the marriage as either decision will be a hard road. Don't leave any question in your mind if this is what you want to do."

I wrote a list of my fears and began to address them one by one. This was the beginning of unwinding the masculine as I had known it. Marriage was forever, right?

The final moment came when I asked James to read this book that I had read on the beach in Hawaii, which was about how couples all operate uniquely. It was by a male author about relationships and spirituality, and he addressed how relationships can change when you begin to awaken to your inner feminine. It was like an ah-ha moment for me about how you love each other and how you begin to recognize that when it's over and that it's completely okay to give yourself permission and be done.

My biggest fear was losing my girls, and part of that fear came to life in the process. It was more like my inner knowing was forewarning me what was coming. I knew that if I stayed in the marriage that I would die as my heart truly yearned to be loved in a way that I had not yet been loved by a man. Furthermore, I yearned to love myself in a way that I hadn't even begun to explore. This was one of the biggest and most painful lessons of my life, but I knew that I had to persevere through it all and see what was on the other side. I knew that I would die otherwise as I almost had with my pulmonary emboli moving through my heart, giving me a giant wake-up call. I knew I wanted to live and be there for my girls versus being buried six feet under from being afraid to choose *me*.

Once I had solidified that I was choosing me, I hired a family divorce lawyer through the help of my high school lawyer friend Robert. I had interviewed a few divorce lawyers before I found the right fit. Don't be afraid to interview those that are doing business for you. I gave my lawyer the retainer and asked him to proceed with the intent to separate.

This was a big decision, and it didn't come easy. I actually pondered this decision for a couple of years before I truly took action. You see, it's not like you plan the date that you will hire a lawyer and proceed with a divorce. Clarity always comes with time, observance, and a deep inner knowing.

My husband and I had been living separate for eighteen months, and I had begun the divorce process. I have always been an active person in my life through figure skating, volleyball, swimming, and HIIT training. I continued to exercise regularly during the entire process as I knew the importance of moving your body through stressful situations to help you cope and reduce your stress levels. There were days when I was literally knocked down by the thought of leaving my marriage and the ranch. I remember walking outside and lying down on the gravel road as my soon-to-be ex-husband drove up, and we ended up in yet another heated disagreement. I was just struck by grief, and I couldn't move. I had many days like this when I would hike the big hills behind our family home on the ranch, and I would lie down on the ground, watching the birds in the sky, listening to nature, crying to myself for hours on end. I even had thoughts of taking my own life at the top of the hill so I could escape the deep pain that I was feeling. I was lucky to have a couple of amazing friends who were counselors and I called them from the top of that hill many times, sharing my dark thoughts with each of them.

During this process, I also went to see my family doctor weekly. I have known her for over twenty-five years as I used to work with her at one of the hospitals in a town close to our ranch, and she had delivered my girls. When I first went in for a follow-up visit after my stay in the critical care unit, she talked to me about my stress levels and also asked me if I felt that I needed to go on medication to help me through the divorce process. She informed me that what I was going through was major and that if I wasn't going to be on medication to help that, I needed to share my plan with her to show her that I would be supported through the process. I told her that I was seeing a counselor and that I would exercise, meditate, reach out to my friends and family when I needed to and that I would commit to seeing her weekly until she felt that I was okay. The work that I do is all about getting to the root cause of the pain and treating it energetically to dissolve the deep roots that began the symptomatic process that shows up within the organs associated with the chakra. I have combined my wisdom of Eastern medicine with Western medicine, and I was going to do exactly this as it is my true belief in all life.

As I moved my way through the grief cycle in unwinding my marriage, I also took a weekend course that was about moving through divorce by Howard and Kerry Parsons. It had a spiritual flair to it, which piqued my interest. I asked my good friend Tracey to take it with me as we were moving through the divorce cycle in similar timing.

I finally had finished my dating profile and had uploaded a few photos of myself that I felt somewhat confident in. I was nervous to see what the next step would be. I began to learn to navigate myself around this dating app that I had chosen to use. I started off with just one dating site. Within a few hours, I began to receive notifications that I had e-mails from potential dates waiting for me in my inbox. I was overwhelmed and shocked to be honest. I didn't expect so many e-mails within a short period. I began to respond to each one of them thinking, that I had to be polite and answer each one. I continued on a few conversations with a few different men whom I felt were kind and with whom I was attracted to. I actually had drawn one of my oracle cards from my deck to use that name as my profile name for the dating site. I didn't want to use my real name for security reasons.

I had an ex-boyfriend, Shane, whom I had dated when I was about nineteen to twenty years old, e-mail me, asking why I was on a dating site. I informed him that yes, I was single now and was going through the divorce process. He asked me to meet him for a drink at his house so we could catch up. He lived only a twenty-minute drive from our ranch. I said I would think about it and get back to him.

I decided to go ahead and meet my ex-boyfriend Shane for a drink as he felt safe, and I thought that this would be a good place to start reconnecting to the male species again. You see, being married for so long, I forgot that I could have male friends. In high school, I had a lot of amazing male friends, and then when I got married, I let all those friendships go because I was under the belief that you can't have friends of the opposite sex when you are married as it will lead to temptation. Not sure where I picked that up, but it was definitely in my awareness.

Luke had sent me an e-mail on the dating app. We had been chatting through the dating app for a few weeks before he asked me to meet for a drink. I had experienced a pulmonary embolism in February 2016 and had to have a follow-up VQ, scan which is a precise CAT scan of the lungs with radioactive dye to check to see if the two emboli were dissolved by the medication that I had been taking for three months. He sent me a message when I returned home from the exam, asking me how my day was. I pondered if I should be vulnerable with him and share my recent cardiac history. I decided to tell him that I had a really bad headache from the radioactive dye and that it wasn't the best day. As soon as I told him why I had the VQ scan done, he said, "Here is my cell number. Please text me as I have had a similar experience."

In previous months, I had a psychic reading, and she had told me that the reason that I had a pulmonary embolism was to take part of a soulmate's pulmonary embolism so he didn't die in this lifetime. I froze when I heard Luke share his story with me that he too had a postoperative pulmonary embolism and almost died. In my head, I was thinking, *Is this the man that I am supposed to be with for the rest of my life? How could this be?*

I had felt an instant connection to him when had talked on the phone the first night. We had talked until the wee hours of the morning for weeks before we actually planned to meet in person.

Luke asked me out on a date the same night that I had planned to meet my Shane, my ex-boyfriend. I told Luke that I could meet in the following weekend as I had already made plans for that night.

It was easy and comfortable connecting with Shane. He wrapped his arms around me and gave me a huge hug, which was just what I needed at that point, a little nurturing from a man I trusted. We talked for hours and got caught up on the last twenty-four years since we had last seen each other.

I continued texting and talking with Luke. I was taking a spiritual postdivorce course the following weekend to help shift through the grief cycle with my girlfriend Tracey. The course began on a Thursday evening, and the instructors had asked us not to date during the course and to wait until Sunday when we were complete. They had advised us that there would be some deep processing that would come forth during these few days. They were absolutely correct. We did a ceremony where we had to face a partner in the course and write a letter to our ex-spouses, thanking them for the gifts that they had brought into our lives and then visualize leaving their hand at the end of the aisle where we had married them. They had played a song that had stirred up deep emotion within myself as I visualized myself letting go of James's hand forever. To this day, this visual still stirs a lump in my throat. I shed some deep ugly cry tears during these few days but also realized that divorce isn't for the faint of heart and that this deep emotional work would pay off in my future relationships.

Luke had agreed to wait until my course was over on Sunday to meet for our first date. I was excited to meet him as we had deeply connected via telephone and texting already, but now the next step of seeing each other would be the greatest test. We had agreed to meet at a local lounge the Sunday afternoon after the course had concluded.

I told him what vehicle I would be driving, and he said that he would be waiting out front of the lounge for me. I was so nervous driving to the location. I had even contemplated having a shot of tequila along the way to calm my nerves. My friend Tracey was with me for part of the drive as we had carpooled to the divorce course together. She said, "I can go with you if you would like?"

I generously declined as I knew that I had to work through my nervous energy myself and that I wouldn't die going on a first date from being nervous.

As I pulled up to park, I saw this tall man with sunglasses walk toward my vehicle. I paused for a moment as Luke had put in his profile that he worked out five times a week, and this man didn't represent that to me. He smiled at me as I opened my vehicle door, and then I knew that it was him for sure. I thought, *Okay, Dawn, just give this a chance as you have made a good connection with Luke already, so be open to seeing how this first meeting goes.*

Once again, my inner knowing was strongly raising one red flag with the dishonesty about the working out.

We walked into the lounge and sat at a table for two, away from everyone else. We ordered drinks, and I began to observe his physical attributes. He had beautiful eyes, and his soul seemed gentle and kind. He reached across the table and asked if he could hold my hand to see if either one of us felt a connection like we had talked about on the phone last week.

I had a dream one night that the man I would end up in a serious relationship next after James, that I would feel his energy in the room before I actually saw him. In this dream, this man would walk up beside me and would hold my hand, and I would feel a surge of loving energy run from my hand into my heart chakra. I had shared this dream with Luke, and I had said that I was looking for affirmation of this dream with that man and had wondered if he was that man.

When our hands connected, I did feel a warm connection, and it made me think that maybe he was this man from my dream. We began to connect for a few hours, talking and asking each other questions about our lives. There was a lot of chemistry between us right from that initial meeting. I knew that I had to get home as my three girls were at home waiting for me to cook supper.

He kissed me in the parking lot, and I could feel the connection, and it made my heart happy to know that this date could lead to the next one and that the first date after my divorce was officially over. I had survived my nervous stomach. As I drove home, he had sent me a few texts, sharing how he had felt a deep attraction and connection. He then asked when we could have another date.

I continued talking to a few other men on the dating app as I had developed a connection between a few of them and that I had wanted to keep my options open. I found myself feeling that I was doing something wrong when I would go on a date with a man as part of me still felt guilty like I was cheating on my ex-husband-to-be. I would find myself looking around the lounge to see if I knew anyone who would know me. This made sense as I was married for twenty-one years. It was going to take some time to unwind that programming.

My connection to Luke grew stronger, and we decided that we were going to date exclusively, and we deleted our dating accounts.

During the last few years of my marriage to James, the physical touch became distant between us as the verbal, emotional, and physical connections all broke down. When Luke would hold my hand, send loving texts, and call me "sweetheart," it melted my heart. I realized how I had been starved from physical affection in my marriage and that my body was craving that intimate physical connection and positive loving words. When Luke would sit near me during our dates, I could feel the energy between us tingling from my toes to my fingertips. I had been longing for this type of connection for a long time.

I was in the middle of the divorce process as I began dating Luke. I had retained a family law lawyer downtown and was meeting him on a regular basis to begin the separation-of-assets process. I remember meeting Luke after one of those meetings, and I was upset because I had to begin to talk about how James and I were going to begin to split our assets, the girls, and so much more. I felt like the life that we had built together was being ripped apart in pieces. This was all unchartered territory for me. I called Luke on my way home from one of these appointments, and he told me to come over. He held me as I cried and shared my deepest fears with him. He asked me if I was truly ready to be dating during the middle of this divorce process. I knew that this was something that I had to consider. I appreciated the friendship and soft arms to fall into during the difficult times, so could I pull away was the question. Was this healthy for me to be dating in the midst of this emotional warfare?

A month into our dating relationship, we decided to book a hotel for a weekend at a nearby ski resort. We had not been intimate up until this point as he was the first man that I would be sexually intimate with after my husband of twenty-one years. I was nervous yet excited. My girlfriend Kathy was teasing, me telling me that I needed to make sure that I didn't take my granny panties with me for the weekend! I had mixed feelings of being intimate with someone new. As those of you who have been in long-term relationships know, it takes a lot of courage to hop into the sheets with someone new. My confidence wasn't at its peak at this point either, so it truly was a ball of mixed emotions for me.

I was still living on the family ranch when I began dating Luke. My girls weren't a fan of me dating and especially didn't like Luke. When I left the ranch that afternoon to meet Luke, as I was driving through town, my ex-husband James was walking across the street to get the mail. I thought to myself, *Isn't this ironic that he is walking across my path as I am intending to begin a new adventure with another man?*

When I look back now, I realize it was the universe showing me the crossing of our paths will never be complete, but how we close those chapters individually is unique.

As I was driving up to the shop where Luke worked, I was talking with my girlfriend Kathy about how nervous I was about spending the weekend with Luke. I truly have the best girlfriends, always supporting me and laughing with me when I need it. I was patiently waiting for Luke to come out of the office. He sent me a text and said that he was delayed as he had an emergency meeting. I said, "No worries, I will sit and wait."

Thirty minutes later, he came out to my car with his bag and told me that he had just been tired! I was in shock and said, "Well, do you still want to go ahead with the weekend?"

He replied, "Yes, there is nothing that I can do about it this weekend."

In my head, I was thinking, *Okay, universe, what kind of sign is this for me? Should I run now?*

This was a big bombshell in my opinion. Something was being shattered here, and I needed to once again wait for the pieces to fall together.

My adoptive mom was worried that was I going to stay overnight with a strange man for the weekend. I said, "Mom, it's okay, there are lots of people in a hotel, and if I don't feel safe, I will reach out, and I am forty-five years old."

Now the room was booked under my name and my credit card. He had offered to pay for half of the room when we talked about it. This should have been my first red flag! We arrived and had a glass of wine. I could feel my nervous energy skyrocketing. Being a forty-five-year-old woman, who has given birth to three children, has stretch marks from those times, and was in a marriage for twenty-one years, to now being intimate with a new man, this was a lot for my internal calm to remain balanced.

As he grabbed my hand and led me upstairs to the loft, I wanted to turn around and run the other way. Was I ready for this? Deep down inside, I felt like I was cheating on my husband. He was the man I had slept beside for so long. I knew his breathing patterns and everything about him.

As we began kissing, he stood up to take off his T-shirt. Out of the corner of my eye, I could see that he clearly didn't work out five times a week. I saw his body, which wasn't matching his dating profile description, and I felt this deep sense of panic inside. You see, I had promised myself that the next man with whom I would be in relationship would take care of his physical body in terms of eating healthy, exercising, having no addictions, and balancing work and rest. Having gone through my own health crisis, I was committed to taking even better care of myself, so I knew I needed a partner who would support this lifestyle. Now I was already partially emotionally invested in Luke, so I chose to live in denial about what I had just seen out of the corner of my eye. I also began to have suspicions that he spent more time that he initially shared with me about being in the bar atmosphere drinking alone.

My first sexual experience with Luke was short and not what I had hoped. It was quick, and I was still having flashbacks of the visual of the T-shirt moment. Having the courage to leave my marriage, I had hopes of the sexy masculine body! I still felt the deep emotional heart connection and told myself that I would hold space and see how I felt about this weekend. Luke held me all night and fell asleep on my pillow, snoring loudly. I didn't sleep a wink all weekend. I was exhausted, and I felt guilty inside. What was I thinking? How could I do this to my family? Was this what I wanted? Was this the greener grass?

As the weekend progressed, we did go for a short hike but spent most the weekend in bed or in the lounge. As we drove home from the weekend, I began to acknowledge that I was craving emotional and physical attention. I also had a deep sense that I was ignoring some "must haves" on my newly developed relationship list that my counselor had me derive. Call me old-fashioned, but I know that I want to be treated like a lady. This weekend hadn't quite gone like I had envisioned.

As I moved through the legal proceedings of my separation from James, I looked to Luke for support. James and I began the mediation process, which involved each of our lawyers and a neutral lawyer who would act as a mediator. We agreed to use a mediator to move through our separation agreement. As we sat in mediation around a huge boardroom table, with James and his lawyer on one side and myself and my lawyer on the other side, I had a huge ah-ha moment. James would lose his temper during the mediation process, and his lawyer would have to remove him to another room until he had cooled off. I looked at my lawyer and said this is one of the reasons that we are getting divorced as this anger wasn't healthy for me. As James's lawyer was trying to shred my personality traits to pieces, I thought to myself, *What must have happened to her as a child for her to be able to treat another person like this?*

Here we are, two people who loved each other, had three amazing daughters together, and created an amazing life together, and now you are trying to break down every ounce of our lives to prove that your client is righteous in his needs.

I just sat back and pondered what is wrong with this scenario. When people are done with their relationships, then just be done. It's time to let go of the ego part of judgment and who gets what. As my lawyer told me from the beginning, "No one wins in divorce. Let's just make it as fair as we can."

In front of you are two people who started off with a good intention to create a family together and a future. Years down the road, choices and evolvement created another path in the future. Sometimes we don't grow together but apart, having our fixed views of what each sees as a possible future. The system is old and can be truly painful to move through when unwinding your marriage. Hence, the reason I am also called to create a workshop to help those who have gone through a relationship ending or divorce. I see a huge need to support in this area to align with those who are spiritually evolving and don't fit into the old legal system.

One day after mediation, I was feeling heartbroken and deeply shaken by all the emotions I was feeling. As soon as I walked out of the office building, I called Luke from my cell phone. As soon as I heard his voice, I began to cry. He said, "Oh, someone is calling on the other line, and I have to go."

I remember that I was walking across the crosswalk, and he hung up on me. I thought to myself, *Okay, Dawn, this is a huge red flag.*

I walked to my car and called my good friend Randy. I was crying deeply and told him what had happened. He was listening and supporting me through it. In the back of my mind, I knew that what Luke had just shown me was the true reality of what I would get in the future, if I chose to go down this road with him. I had many moments like this driving from mediation downtown back to the ranch where I was living still.

The months went by, and my gut feelings were confirmed about Luke spending a lot of time in the bar drinking alone. I confronted him about it, and he broke up with me, telling me that it was none of my business where he spent his time. This was about two months into the relationship. I remember crying in my closet, almost begging him not to break up with me because I couldn't have one more person reject me. I hung up the phone and felt as if my walls were crumbling down around me.

As this moment, I didn't have the self-confidence to leave this dating relationship. I continued to see the red flags through alcohol abuse, emotional abuse, and old childhood wounds rearing up without any consideration of accountability.

We continued to date on and off for almost three years. Our relationship was always in turmoil, and he was threatening to break up with me. It was very unstable and not at all what I should have been in during this grief cycle after a twenty-one-year marriage.

I think we knew that, but neither of us wanted to let each other go, so we continued the unhealthy attachment-style relationship for way too long. I continued to go to counseling through it all, and she would always refer me back to my original must-have, can't-have, and absolute-no spreadsheet of what I needed from a relationship. I chose to live in denial.

I think part of me felt like I didn't deserve to be happy as I was the one who wanted to end my marriage and that I had torn my family apart. An unhealed part of myself felt that I deserved to be punished for my actions. Yes, I know, not realistic or healthy, but it was my mindset.

We had purchased an engagement ring earlier on in the relationship from a very prestigious jewelry store. He had paid for half, and I had paid for half. Yes, another red flag to add to my collection already. I had even inquired if we could return the ring as I had just seen too much and no change.

When I brought this up, Luke cried and said that he wanted to change his unhealthy lifestyle but needed some help. So he began seeing a psychologist. The appointments weren't consistent, and it seemed like there was a lot of projection coming my way versus accountability, so I wasn't convinced that this would work.

One day my counselor said to me, "Dawn, not only are you only pulling the wagon with Luke in it, but he's falling out of the wagon and you are trying to put him back in it while pulling it behind you!"

That was a huge eye-opener for me to see the visual, and truly, the relationship felt very heavy and strained.

My dad had mentioned to me that we should move in together for a few months and that it would become very clear very soon if we could continue this relationship. I had this thought flowing through my mind often.

I was accused of cheating on Luke with almost every male person I would connect with, from the home-builder to the realtor, etc. I never once cheated on Luke while we were dating, so I wasn't sure where he was getting this vibe from, but it was destroying any chance of trust that we might have.

All my friends and family would tell me that they would support me with whatever decision I made to stay with Luke or end the relationship. Some would speak up very strongly and tell me that they didn't like him, that he wasn't good for me, and that I deserved to be treated better. I knew this deep in my soul, but the illusionist within me wanted to give him a million chances.

Then near Christmas, three years into the on-and-off dating scenario, he proposed to me with the ring that we had bought together in my living room. I remember thinking, *I need to say* no *to marrying this man*, but I wasn't strong enough to say no yet. Maybe he would change. Maybe we would be happy. Maybe he truly loved me and was just blowing off steam frequently. Maybe not.

He moved in for three weeks after the proposal, and that was all it took to get the clarity that I needed that this relationship was done for me. I needed to honor my needs that I had so carefully thought out with my counselor. I needed to gather the strength and end this once and for all.

We had continuous fighting while we lived together, and my cardiologist had told me that I needed to live with low stress in my life from that day forward if I could avoid it. So I asked him to move out and to give me some space to get clarity from the anger and projection. I took off the engagement ring and put it back into the box. I knew that I would be betraying myself if I followed through with this.

We began to see each other less and less, and I continued to my counseling. I had just built a new home, so I had plenty of projects to keep myself busy during this time. He was begging me to not cut him out of my life. I kept asking the universe for signs that I was doing the right thing!

A girlfriend of mine came over for tea one day, and she asked me if Luke and I were still together. I said, "Well, we are working on things but see each other casually. Why do you ask?"

She said, "Well, I am pretty sure that I saw his dating profile on a dating app, and he was online two days ago!"

I was in shock. He wouldn't do this to me after all that we have been through, would he? I anxiously waited for my friend to leave so I could create a fake dating account on that app, so I could see if she was telling me the truth!

I thought to myself, *He better not be on here*, and voila! About twenty men through the filtering process, there he was!

He even wrote in his paragraph about himself the same line that he used to propose to me about love! Wow, that stung! I saw photos of our travels together when he would lean away to take a selfie of himself when I was sitting right beside him, and my gut was telling me that he would use these photos on his dating profile one day down the road, and I was correct! He even had a headshot of him standing outside my house in Hawaii at Christmas. I was so hurt and shocked.

I called him instantly and asked him if he had anything to tell me. He said, "No!"

I said, "Really? Well, why are you on a dating app?"

Boom! That was the end. I kept asking the universe for a bold sign to help me finally leave this unhealthy relationship, and there it was!

I have a football length of red flags from this relationship to last me a lifetime. It was a two-way street here for accountability. My lesson with Luke was that I should have never been dating anyone during my grief cycle postdivorce. I would advise anyone who is fresh out of a long-term relationship or marriage to be single for a long time until you have moved through the entire process of grieving. It's not fair to you or the person you are dating.

I also feel that the vibration that I was putting out into the universal force field of dating was shattered and broken, which is exactly what I had attracted into my life. When you are grieving, you can't think clearly and aren't equipped to make good decisions.

Do I regret my decisions along the way with Luke? Yes, I do. If you go back to the first initial date, where he wasn't honest with his appearance, that is when I should have said goodbye and moved on. I was not thinking clearly and had a lot to heal within myself. We were supposed to be together for a reason, but the lesson just kept repeating itself over and over because I was not conscious of a healthy relationship at the time.

If you see those red flags, look at them. Make sure that your must-have relationship list is complete and honor every aspect of what you need from a relationship because you deserve it. Don't ever settle for less than what you want!

CHAPTER 3

Drive-By

Name: Jackson
Occupation: Analyst
Age: 45
Height: 5'8"

First date out of the gate!

I always have an intention for every action that I take in my life. Before I went to the online dating sites, I made some intentions: a man who has his financial house in order, one who takes care of his physical body, has a healthy relationship with his mother and children, is open to travel, has a healthy sex drive, isn't abusive, has an open mind, and gets along with my friends and family.

Next step was to set up on my own profile. I channeled what I was looking for and then added photos of myself that I felt good in. Then I had to set up my age range, likes, and preferences.

This took a bit, but I wanted to set up a solid foundation with a healthy awareness anchoring in my intentions.

Online dating can have a bad rep for sure as can everything in life. My view is that your intention is key in all that you do. Your outer world is a reflection of your inner world. I don't buy into others' external views most times and certainly not with dating.

I decided that I would start with two different dating websites. I am a forty-eight-year-old woman who has had three children and honestly didn't know what to expect.

As the e-mails came in on the two apps, I began to wonder if I was going to be attracted to any of these men. I have to say that I was a bit discouraged at first. I wasn't looking for a seventy-one-year-old man with a beer belly, so why was this an option for them to contact me?

As I view each photo, I can feel the energy of each man. I can feel if they are a real person or if they are a computer-generated catfisher. I can even feel the chakras if I spend enough time tapping into their auric field. This is a perk of my job!

The first man who caught my eye was Jackson. His smile lights up the photo, and his eyes have this mischievous inviting twinkle to them. I then looked at his profile closer, looking at his height, occupation, education, if he is a nonsmoker, and if he has children. I decided that he ticked off enough of my "must have" boxes and made the first move and messaged him. In his profile, he stated that he wanted to be a sommelier, and this was something that drew me into conversation with him. I ask him if he prefers red or white. He answers with red. I then ask what blend of red. He answers with malbec, and I answer with old vine zinfandel.

The conversation then opens up into getting to know each other. How long have you been divorced? Do you have children, and if so, how many, and what are their ages? We talk daily for a few days and then exchange cell phone numbers to further the dating connection. I am attracted to this man's photo, and I am wondering, *Is he real? Is my intuition guiding me down the wrong path? Will he be attracted to a woman who is forty-eight years old when he is forty-five years old?*

He asks if we can talk on the phone one evening. I can feel myself freeze inside! I want to keep it on the surface via texting. I realize the invitation to connect deeper is a trigger for me. Why do I want to keep this on the surface? What is it within me that is fearful of talking with Jackson? I am a confident woman, so what the hell is this thought running through my head?

We make a time to talk when his children are in bed and we can have some privacy. I am excited yet nervous. I call him and hear his voice for the first time. He sounds like a confident man with a sense of mischief about him as I saw in his eyes from his photo. We talk briefly but then have to go as his daughter wakes up and has been trying to listen to him around the corner. I smile to myself, thinking how it must be a balancing act being a single dad raising children and trying to date.

We continue getting to know each other via phone calls and texts over the next few weeks. Each time my cell phone would light up with his name on the display, I would feel like a schoolgirl anxiously awaiting the "boy" to call.

I found, as I began to explore this relationship with Jackson, that I was going to be my authentic self, no holding back. So he was truly my first experience in sexting before I met him in person. I thought, *This is weird*, that I am sharing these deep sexual thoughts with a man I haven't met yet.

I could feel the sexual desire building between our texts and phone calls. It made me truly wonder what it would be like to meet him in person.

We then set the evening for our first date. I invited him to come for a glass of wine to my house, where we could sit and get to know each other on a deeper level. Meanwhile, my girlfriends were losing their minds about my physical safety with a strange man in my home. I kept telling them that I live my life using my inner GPS, that I trusted this man, and that I would be okay. If I needed help, then I would seek it.

My girlfriend Christina said, "If you need a backup plan, just text me a 911, and I will show up with my bag, and I will be crying, saying, 'My boyfriend kicked me out, and I need a place to stay!'"

As I nervously waited for him to show up, I was a nervous wreck. I felt like a fifteen-year-old going on my first date again at forty-eight. I had so many thoughts going through my mind: What if he thinks I look too old? Will that first kiss be awkward? And will he look like his profile and photos had stated? I have heard many stories of people who lie about their height, age, and physical appearance on their profiles.

As time went by, hc sent me a text me and said that he was having a technical glitch with a program at work and that he was going to be delayed a bit. I took a deep breath and let out a sigh of relief because that gave me more time to avoid the first meeting. Then as hours went by, I sent a text message, asking him if he was still coming. Crickets. No response.

Stood up! First date and a no-show. Now I am the good old-fashioned small-town farm girl who would never not show up without letting the other person know. So my mind began to create different scenarios of what must have happened for Jackson to not show up that evening. It was snowing that night, so I figured that maybe he had been in an accident! I lay awake all night, worrying about his well-being.

The next morning, I sent one of my psychic friends a text with Jackson's photo, asking her to tell me if he as alive or not. Her response was quick and firm. Yes, he's okay, but he's depressed about his ex-wife. She said he couldn't show up for you because he is still in love with her.

I was relieved to know that he was okay but have to say that I was disappointed in his accountability for not letting me know. Two days later, I received this lengthy text with an apology from Jackson, explaining that he should have let me know, etc. We set up another date. I have to say that I was skeptical at this point, having been stood up once before, but I appreciated his honest text explaining why he hadn't shown up. Second date set, but then he tells me that he can't make it work.

At this point, I begin to doubt my intuition, and I wonder if he does actually exist! I begin to feed my own fears with external stories from others to validate that online dating is hard and time-consuming.

Jackson continues to respond with an apology and that he does want to meet. So we set up a third date and time. Yes, I am doubtful that he will show up. I am mad at myself for not dumping his ass the first no-show! I decide that I have nothing to lose by meeting him, but this is the last time that I will be stood up.

He texts me to tell me that he is on his way to my house and that he will be there in exactly nineteen minutes according to his Google maps. I pace the floor while talking to my girlfriend Patti. I keep walking into my daughter's bedroom to look out her window to watch for his vehicle. Soon I see a gray truck pull into my driveway, and my nervous energy is at its all-time high. He rings the doorbell, and I slowly open my door to keep my dog Laila inside of the house. I peek around the door and see his amazing eyes shining right at me. I smiled and said, "Oh, you are real."

As he walked in through the door, we gently embraced with a hug. I can smell his cologne and feel his body strong against mine. I knew from our previous texts that we would have a strong sexual chemistry. We sat down on my leather couch across each other, talking and getting to know each other. He was easy to talk to too, and my eyes were devouring his physical attributes. He had a warm beautiful smile and a witty sense of humor. He is an Aries like I am, and I could feel the fire burning hot between the two of us as we connected. He had a cold, and he didn't want to risk giving it to me, so we never kissed on that first meeting, only an embrace. We talked about how he never showed up on the two previous dates. I was teasing him about how I was starting to second-guess if he was real or not.

We continued to talk via phone and over text and made plans to meet for our second date. I was scared that my sexual feelings for Jackson would override my morals. He was an attractive man, and through texting, we had already shared some of our deepest sexual desires for each other. When he arrived at the door, for the first time, he kissed me with a passionate kiss, and I could smell the cologne as I buried my face into his neck. I could feel his strong arms around me. The combination of his strength and cologne melted my body. All I could think about was physically acting out our sexual desires that we had shared via text.

As he held my hands on the couch, and we talked on a deeper level, I knew that I wasn't going to be able to resist this urge if it was presented. We talked about his work and my work and began that deeper-friendship connection. He admitted that he knew nothing about my spiritual work but was keen to know more about it.

I could feel the fire inside of myself when I thought of Jackson. My sexual chemistry was stirring with thoughts of us. There is nothing like an attractive man who smells good to start those sexual endorphins flowing for me. He was smart, active, an amazing dad to his children, and has his financial house in order. Bam! Just what I was intending, right? The universe had delivered him express to my doorway.

Then the time came when I knew I was going to have to allow myself to own my sexuality as a forty-eight-year-old woman. I knew that I couldn't fight my sexual chemistry with him and that I had to surrender to the feelings and desires that I was having. I was fighting old paradigms in my head, that it was wrong to surrender to these thoughts so early on in a relationship, that it was not okay that we had to put more time into our relationship before we could enjoy the pleasures of each other's bodies.

Too many times in my life have I stuck to the rigged man-made belief systems and denied my own heart. I promised myself after breaking my engagement off with Luke that I would follow my heart and soar in freedom in a reasonably responsible way. This was my moment to choose. Was I going to shrink to conform to those old box structures, or was I going to break open that old mold through my heart?

I allowed my heart to lead the way. I grabbed his hand and led him upstairs to my bedroom. I craved for him to be naked against me, feeling his skin against mine, smelling his cologne, melting into each other. He was very much a gentleman, never pushing my boundaries, always asking me if I was okay with what was happening. My hand explored his hard chest muscles as I admired the physical work that he puts into his body. In my head, I was thinking I have always wanted a man who takes care of his body and that this is a definite plus to "must haves" on my checklist.

As he started to kiss me and our naked bodies were against each other, I could feel my nervous tension melting into the passion of our bodies wanting each other. I had some insecurities flowing through my mind as I am forty-eight years old and my body isn't as it used to be.

He was an amazing lover, making sure that I was pleased first and foremost. My body had moved in ways that it hadn't ever! The strong sexual chemistry was fluent in our sexual actions. The fluidity of following my heart was evident in the sexual connection. As my mind tried to induce guilt that I had done something wrong according to the old act of sexual interaction, if there is such a thing, I kept going back to the sense of freedom and excitement that I was feeling. This was the first time that I had truly allowed myself to feel pleasure without the rigid paradigms of the past. I started to ponder where did I begin to have this belief instilled within me. Then I remembered my mother telling me when I was date-raped at fifteen years old that I should have waited until I was married to have sex, that I would be lucky if anyone wanted to date me now that this had occurred. I felt scarred a long time after this.

I realized that I was still controlled by this old paradigm and that I was the only one who could abolish it. I told myself that when I started dating again, this time around I wouldn't look to my friends and family for validation in the person or process. I truly wanted to experience from the inside out my relationship with the divine masculine as an expanded woman. The process of sorting through these old beliefs was just the beginning of my own divine masculine awakening. You see, we all have the divine feminine and divine masculine within each of us.

Jackson sent me a text one day shortly after we had connected and said that he began to realize that he wasn't ready for a serious relationship. He told me that he still goes to counseling and that he had thought that he had worked through all his stuff from his ex but clearly he hadn't.

My first reaction was to take this personally. It must be me that he was rejecting. He reassured me that I was an amazing woman and that he would regret doing this but that he wasn't ready to commit to a relationship. Now my old natural pattern of codependency is to always be in a relationship to feel safe. I was flattered that he acknowledged that I was an amazing woman, but then the flip side of the ego was telling me that somehow I was flawed.

We had such a strong connection physically and a gentle friendship that was growing. I distanced myself from Jackson for a few weeks but thought of him often, and we continued to text. I love a man with a good healthy banter. Jackson is an Aries, so he can give the sarcasm back to me like I dish it out to him. It's a playful witty exchange that lights my fire. Many times I will address him by his surname for play.

I truly began to ponder my own intentions during this process apart. I began questioning my old belief systems that I had to have one committed relationship to be a good law-abiding citizen. Who the hell makes up this crap, and why was I thinking it in my mind?

As I processed my own inner dialogue, I reached out to Jackson and explained to him my thought process. He concurred but once again shared that he wasn't ready to have a committed relationship and that he didn't want to hurt me. I like to get to the root of all things in life. My mind was curious as to what did he still needed to work through to be in a relationship, and/or was it truly just me that he felt no spark with?

I asked him why he went on a dating website when he didn't want to commit. He then confided in me that he didn't realize that he still had fear until we had met. I asked him, "What is your biggest fear in committing to another relationship?"

He said that he was afraid of making the same mistakes as he had done in his marriage of seven years. He was afraid to give that "soulmate" love to another again and to be rejected himself. He said marriage is a once-in-a-lifetime kind of love where you marry your soulmate. He said that he loved being married and now the illusion of marriage has been tainted for him. Jackson said that he feels that he will never fully commit to that level again.

I asked him what his intention was for online dating. He said it truly was to find love again and not for a hook-up. He admitted that he may be self-sabotaging, looking or finding fault in a woman without a fair chance because of the greater fear of being vulnerable, hurt, and rejected.

He also said that he is constantly comparing values that don't align with his marriage and that this is a reason to shut down and pull away.

He also said that he enjoys spending time with his children a week on, and then on his week off, he loves to play baseball, golf, and spending time with his buddies. He said, "I like my freedom of not having to answer to anyone, and I don't know if I will ever do that again."

I can so relate to this feeling and ponder that thought a lot myself. Society can create judgment regarding the level of commitment in a sexual relationship. This is part of the paradigm that I wish to bust. It can create segregation and a feeling of confinement.

I can't be on any form of hormonal birth control because of my history of having a pulmonary embolism in February 2016. So I knew that this could be an issue in the dating world. I was grateful to hear that Jackson had a vasectomy. I do practice safe sex, and I value the importance of my health. When I missed my period for a whole month, I was thinking that it was one of two things, that perimenopause had begun or that I was pregnant. I kept this to myself, thinking what I am going to do at forty-eight years old. My youngest daughter is sixteen years old. I wasn't prepared to begin a family again at this age, nor do I think it's a healthy decision for anyone. So when Jackson sent me a text one afternoon on his way home from work, asking me how my day was, I replied with, "Well, the good news is that I am not pregnant."

My phone rang instantly! He said, "What?" He said, "Why didn't you tell me that you were worried about being pregnant?"

And I said, "Because I'm pretty sure that it wasn't possible with my age, your vasectomy, and the use of protection."

I appreciate his concern and quick action to make sure that I was okay.

These wounds from divorce can be buried deep for a lifetime for many. Falling in love and getting married is a very vulnerable process. Many times, when a man has removed his armor for marriage, it is for life. The realization of the pain of losing someone you love can armor you up again for the rest of your life, man or woman. Personally, I would rather feel pain than feel nothing at all. Loving is one of the greatest gifts we are given.

As I began to reevaluate my own morals, I also began to explore the question of, did I want to have another committed relationship myself? I have been dating in a committed relationship since I was fifteen years old. I truly began looking at why I had done this type of relationship. Of course, being married for twenty-one years and having the courage to leave the marriage was a very long and committed process. Then moving into an engagement for another three years with a very controlling man certainly heightened my sense of commitment.

I feel some past-life karmic connection to Jackson. The moment that I first saw him, I knew his soul; hence, the instant comfort level with him and deep sexual chemistry.

After much contemplation, I decided to continue to follow my heart and just flow with my connection to Jackson. He will be my only drivebyyyc. I use this term with him because when we need to physically connect with each other, we say that it's time for a drive-by. Our relationship isn't just a sexual connection, and I want to clarify that. We text often and share our personal issues with each other. I was in deep mediation, and my spirit guides showed me that he had a broken heart energetically and that I was helping him heal from this as he is helping me heal from my pain with past men.

I truly embraced my sexuality with Jackson. I told him that I am going to do the things on my bucket list as I am halfway through life, and if I don't do it now, when will I? I remember Oprah saying that she loved being fifty years old because this is the age that women are that their sexual prime with confidence and an understanding of their bodies. I have to agree with her, the closer that I am getting to fifty years old. Being confident is sexy to men. Owning your body and knowing what you want and need are powerful tools in expressing your sexual freedom.

Jackson will always hold a special place in my heart for the gift of allowing me to express my innermost sexual desires and to just be me with him. He represents a good portion of the divorced men who are truly afraid to be vulnerable in another relationship again. They don't know how to release the pain and heal the heart pain to be vulnerable in another relationship. Men tend to think in black and white, there is no gray area, so releasing the old pain may never happen. What we need to help men with is exactly this: removing the armor and being vulnerable to trust again.

CHAPTER 4

Take It Slow

Name: Mark
Occupation: Director of operations
for commercial oil and gas
Age: 47
Height: 5'10"

Stepping out of my comfort with the bad boys!

Throwback to when the charming man would beat the bad boy!

My girlfriends and I took a hot holiday to Hawaii for a couple of weeks to enjoy the sunshine and the ocean. My one girlfriend Kathy said, "Show me how this online dating works?"

She has been married for over twenty years and said that she was living vicariously through me. Many of my girlfriends who are in marriages or committed relationships often said to me. They are always asking me who is in my inner dating circle and to please share the deets!

As we were scrolling through the options of potential male candidates, I came across Mark. I was attracted to his gentle smile, warm eyes, and clean suit. The instant connection to him was the fact that he stated in his profile that he loved Hawaii! Bingo! A man with the same love for the island as myself, I had to pursue this.

A good part of my dating history is to always be drawn toward the bad boys or the rebels—the men who have that bad-boy sex appeal that your parents don't want you to date in high school! I usually go for those men!

Mark wore a suit and worked downtown in the hustle and bustle, which really enhanced my desire to seek the connection of a clean-cut, sexy man. You see, being married to a cattle rancher for twenty-one years, this was quite the opposite of what I knew. My curiosity got the best of me, and I sent him a message regarding our mutual love for Hawaii.

He was quick to respond. He asked if he could call me while I was in Hawaii. Once again, I froze inside, panicking, thinking of an excuse not to talk with him over the phone. I was processing in my mind why I was so scared to verbally connect with Mark. Was it the next step of intimacy that scared me? I was seeing a pattern within myself that I kept trying to keep the conversation only through text, which, in my mind, keeps the communication on the surface, and I am safer this way.

Kathy said to me, "Just call him; you have nothing to lose!"

So I agreed to talk with him on the phone, feeling the female support of my girl tribe with me in Hawaii. His voice was deep and sexy. We easily connected, talking about which Hawaiian Islands we have been to and which ones we loved the most. He offered to pay for the phone call if it had cost me anything extra. I was happily surprised by his generosity as I had rarely experienced this from a man other than my dad.

I felt a wave of connection inside of me with Mark and was looking forward to getting to know him more. We continued to text while I was away, and I talked to him one more time from the beach, where we made plans to have a glass of wine two days after I returned home.

He had asked me what kind of wine I liked, and I replied with, "I love an old vine zinfandel."

He shared that he enjoyed a nice glass of cabernet sauvignon. I once again invited him to come to my house to meet and have our first date. My girlfriends were reading me the riot act again about my safety. This was me following my gut feeling again, avoiding the external concern.

Once again, I was on the phone with my girlfriend Kathy when I saw a black truck pull into my driveway. I eagerly made my way downstairs to greet him at my door. He had an amazing smile with gentle blue eyes. We greeted each other with a gentle embrace. He as a well-dressed man with beautiful brown dress shoes and a tailored dressed shirt. I don't know why these details are important to some women, but they just are. The first impression can mean a lot, and this certainly was a good one.

He had brought me a bottle of old vine zinfandel! Not his favorite wine but mine! First sign that he was listening and this made my heart happy.

We sat on the loveseat together, enjoying a glass of the wine. We were talking about Hawaii and the things that we loved the most. He was telling me that one day when he retired, he wanted to spend a lot of time in Hawaii. I could hear my soul singing, "Aloha!" You see, I have never traveled to Hawaii with a man and had a successful vacation together. The energy of the island and Pele always seemed to stir up the differences between myself and my ex-husband and ex-fiancé. I always say if you want to know if you should marry the person, take them to Hawaii and see how they do with Pele's goddess energy.

As we began getting to know each other, I mentioned to him in passing that I believed in past lives. He paused for a moment and said, "Wait, you believe in past lives?"

I replied, "Yes, I absolutely do."

I then explained to him my belief in spirit being infinite, like energy, and that you can never destroy it. Mark's father is a retired minister, so I knew that my belief system was going to either repel him or invite him into another way of thinking. He said, "Can you prove why you think this?"

I quickly ran upstairs and found my youngest daughter's Mother's Day scrapbook that she had made for me in kindergarten when she was five years old. I pointed to the page that asked the children what they wanted to be when they grew up, and she said, "I want to be a human with legs."

I shared with him that how could my five-year-old daughter know that she was incarnated and that this was her inner knowing that she had been in spirit form for many lifetimes before, but this was perhaps her first lifetime in a human body. I thought to myself, *Well, this is deep conversation for our first date*, and that I just may have scared him off at this point!

Halfway through the night, he looked me in the eyes and asked if he could kiss me. I replied with, "Well, now I am nervous that you asked, but yes, you sure can."

Mark is a very sensual man. He comes across very confident, like he knows how to treat a lady. We ended the date on a good note, planning for the next date before he went out my front door. I was excited about the possibilities of this first date with Mark. He checked off a lot of the "must haves" on my list!

We met again a couple of nights after our first date. He asked me to come into his place. He lives downtown, in a bigger city. As I was making my way along the forty-minute drive, I decided to call my girlfriend Kathy to distract my mind while I was driving. I found myself nervous like a schoolgirl wanting to impress the teacher. I started to ponder why I felt the need to impress Mark already. Why was I feeling that I couldn't just be myself in his presence?

As I began to get closer to his condo building, I called him, and he gave me the code to access his underground parking. I had some trouble getting the code to work and had a few vehicles waiting behind me, which added to my already-nervous stomach! He said, "Don't worry, I will come down in the elevator and help you."

I finally got the code to work and found the first open guest parking spot and took it! I was relieved and excited to be there. As I looked out my window, there was Mark, smiling, opening my car door, leaning in, and greeting me with a kiss.

I was very attracted to this man and his gentle loving nature toward me. He held my hand, and we walked across the parking lot to the elevator. I felt a natural sense of calm energy when I was holding his hand. He looked me in the eyes as we were going up the elevator, and I could feel this surge of energy run through my body. His eyes were intense. As we made our way up the elevator, he held the door to his condo open for me and took my coat to hang it up. When I turned the corner to see the magnificent view overlooking the city lights, I saw a charcuterie board on the island with two wine glasses. I felt this deep sense of gratitude for the thought that Mark had put into our second date.

I mean, when Luke proposed to me, he made me a charcuterie board after many years, and here I was, on a second date with Mark, and he made this for me! I thought, *What the hell was I doing before with Luke?*

If I had known that there were men out there who treated women like this, I would have exited that relationship a long time ago.

He showed me around his place and asked me which bottle of wine that I would like from his collection. I said, "You choose."

He opened the bottle of wine and poured two glasses, handing me one of them. He looked me in the eyes and said, "Cheers to our second date."

We sat down on two chairs around his island in the kitchen, looking out the floor-to-ceiling windows that overlooked the lights of the downtown city. It was a very romantic setting, and he was a very charming man. He took his finger and slowly caressed my forearm looking into my eyes. He then whispered into my ear, saying, "Where the hell have you been?" and I replied with, "Looking for you."

As we kissed, I could feel the electrical energy run from my lips throughout my body. My mind was whirling with romantic anticipation of what was next.

We sat together at the island, drinking our wine and sharing the charcuterie board. I asked him if he had prepared the board himself or had it prepared by someone else. He said, "It was simple! I just threw it together after work."

I told him that I was impressed at his effort for a second date. We had some deep conversation, and I enjoyed his kissing and caressing of my arms.

He asked me if I wanted to move to the love seat to get more comfortable. In my mind, I knew exactly where this was going, and I wasn't sure how I felt yet. Mark seemed conservative but also wildly romantic. He filled up our glasses of wine and carried them over to the love seat. I was observing how his actions were very nurturing, and this was something that I wasn't used to as a strong Aries woman. When you are married to a cattle rancher, you tend to become pretty self-sufficient as many times I would face obstacles solo as he was out of cell service.

As we were looking into each other's eyes, Mark said to me, "What is this block that I can feel that you have toward me?"

I thought about it for a minute to go inside myself, and he was right, I was guarding myself. I had my guard up because I was hurt in my last relationship. I took a deep breath, and I said, "I need to put my hand on your heart. Is that okay with you?"

He said, "Absolutely, you can do what you need to."

I closed my eyes and placed my left hand on his heart and felt the connection open up between us as he closed his eyes and told me how good it felt to have my hand on his heart. I was thinking, *Well, this man is way more open than I thought that he would be.*

Time went by so fast as we just sat and connected physically while talking, getting to know each other more deeply.

He then asked me to go with him to the bedroom. I told myself that after leaving my long-term marriage, I was going to follow my heart and let go of my own internal judgment regarding male relationships and sex. We spent time just holding each other and kissing. We talked, and then I felt that I needed to go home. He told me that I could spend the night and that nothing would happen sexually if I was uncomfortable with it. I politely declined and made my way to the hall to get my coat. He followed me to the closet where he leaned me against the wall while kissing me passionately. I truly was debating staying with him after feeling the passion from the kissing and caressing. He helped me put on my long white winter coat, and he walked me to the elevator. As we were walking to the elevator, he was kissing me, and I could feel the sexual energy getting stronger between us. We entered into the elevator where he backed me up against the wall in the elevator, pressing his body against mine, kissing me passionately. I truly wanted him to take me right there in the elevator but resisted the urge to be that risky and held his hand as he walked me out to my car.

As I drove home that night, I was excited to meet a man who made me feel like I was a lady for the first time in a very long time. We had planned for him to join me at my house on our next date, where I was going to make him a homemade supper with roast beef, Yorkshire pudding, gravy, and a homemade white chocolate torte cake dessert. The urge to cook for him told me that I was regaining my internal chi for life. The bulk of my life when I was married was devoted to cooking for my family and large gatherings, which I loved to do. This urge was lost for some time as I weaved my way through depression postdivorce and not having anyone to cook for anymore; hence, the elation when I was excited to cook for Mark. This was a good sign.

I had expressed to Mark that when we chose to have a sexual relationship, it was important to me that we spend the night together to respect each other. I knew that time was coming, and possibly, it was this night as I began cooking for him. With a nice bottle of red wine in his hand, he arrived promptly at the time that he had said he would be arriving. He helped me prepare the roast by carving it. We sat and talked as we enjoyed the home-cooked meal. It felt natural to be with him. His smile sent flutters to my heart. After the meal, he poured more wine into our glasses, and we sat on the couch, enjoying each other's company.

We decided that he would spend the night at my house and that we would take that next step in our relationship. He removed his clothes and folded them neatly on the chair in my bedroom while I changed into some sexy lingerie to accommodate the sexual energy exchange that was about to happen between us. I had thought about this moment for some time. I was anticipating this intense sexual experience from the physical caressing and the chemistry that had led up to this moment.

Sometimes the outside doesn't match the inside. This was my first experience of a built-up experience in my head gone the opposite. Let's just say that things weren't as expected. We spent the night together. I was processing my disappointment without sleeping a wink through the night. I was understanding and understood that being in your head can kill the mood instantly. So I was going to "chalk" it up to just that this time. He was up early to head back into the city for his work. I had a coffee and dealt with my inner turmoil of confusion. I had a lot of thoughts going through my mind. Maybe he just wasn't that attracted to me. He had affirmed that this had nothing to do with me at all, so I trusted his word.

I always felt that uncertainty when we parted ways. I had never felt this feeling before in any of my relationships. In those times, I would look within to see if I had any codependence issues still rooted somewhere in my energy that I needed to clear up. Certainly, I did! No surprise, being married for twenty-one years. You naturally can become dependent on each other in long-term relationships. I knew that I must also be picking up on how he was feeling too, being empathic myself.

He had told me that he was married to his work and that it would always be a priority. I have been in this circus before, married to a cattle rancher who rarely takes any hours off. This was a red flag for me for sure. No matter how much I was treated like a lady, being put on the back burner from the get-go was weighing deeply on my heart.

He told me that he wouldn't be able to text during the day because work was so busy. I honored that and could accept that. Until I went to go on my dating app to turn off my profile and had seen that he was active on this app during the day. Now I wanted to deny that this is what I saw, but I knew that I had to address this as it was going to bother me until I had shared my concern. I broached the subject on a date, and he told me that he wasn't actively looking but that he was just passing time like scrolling through social media! Really. I am not that naïve, thank you very much. Another red flag for me. If you didn't have time to text the woman that you were dating during the day, then how could you find the time to scroll through the dating app?

We saw each other a few more times and had a quiet night connecting and just chilling with a glass of wine and a movie. I stayed over at his house and loved to look at the city lights shining in his condo at night. He always treated me like a classy lady.

I have to admit there was passion missing in the bedroom for me. This never did change between us. It felt a bit clinical to me, and I always felt it was because he lived in his head a lot, focusing on his work. A reason the red flag was popping up for me again. Ignoring red flags only causes anxiety for me, so I am not sure why I wasn't addressing the real truth sooner than later. I wanted to wait a bit longer and see if he would shift his priorities the more we got to know each other.

Christmas season was upon us. I was having my annual Christmas party for my alumni, and I asked him to join me to meet some of my friends. He thanked me and told me that he had his annual company Christmas party the same night in a ski town a couple of hours away. I knew that this wasn't going to line up much to my deep disappointment. I had a bought a brand new sexy navy silk dress to wear for my Christmas party! I decided to stick with my plan to dress up and enjoy the party, pushing my disappointment to the side. It was a fun night had by all. There is nothing like a shooter pantry party to get the truth serum flowing. I must admit that I tried to call Mark a few times that evening, but no answer to a call or a text.

Three weeks went by where we didn't see each other, but we did keep in touch through phone calls and texts. I told him that I would love to get dressed up and go out for supper one night to celebrate the Christmas season. We picked a night that we mutually agreed upon. I was excited to dress up and spend time with him over a nice meal. Christmas always means a lot to me.

I did my hair and makeup and slipped on my white silk dress in preparation for our dinner date. I had stopped by the local liquor store and picked up a bottle of nice scotch to give him for Christmas. As I was preparing to leave the house, he sent me a text, saying they had started drinking in the office to celebrate Christmas and that he was a well on his way to being drunk. My heart sank. I could feel the disappointment. I said, "That's okay. I will come and pick you up wherever you are at."

As I made my way onto the highway, the snow was coming down hard and fast. I was driving in a full-on whiteout. I called my friend Kathy from the car phone and asked her to Google the address that Mark was at and to please text me the directions. She asked me why I was still going knowing full well that he was drunk and now I was driving in a blizzard. She was right! I thought to myself, *Why in the hell was I putting myself in this position?* I kept driving and told myself that I would turn around if it got any worse.

As I made my way closer to the downtown destination, he sent me a text, saying he would be outside waiting for me when I was closer. I sat in my vehicle in my white satin dress with my long white coat, watching for him to come outside. He came out of the doors toward my vehicle and slipped on the snow with his dress shoes and fell under my car. I immediately burst out laughing, thinking that I should get out of my vehicle and see if he was okay. Within a minute, he bounced up, opened the passenger door, and said, "I am okay," with a huge smile on his face.

He looked over at me all dressed up, with my bare leg showing, and said, "Maybe we should just go back to my place right now!"

I said, "No, I think that we should get some food and water into you."

We ended up at a classy steak restaurant with live music.

The waitress seated us at a private table. The sommelier came over with a wine list, and Mark told the sommelier that I was to choose the wine. As I perused the wine list, I asked John which bottle he would prefer, and ultimately, I felt that I wanted him to be in charge of choosing. I love to be treated like a lady, but ultimately, I love a man in charge sometimes for the date and in the bedroom. The sommelier came with a cabernet sauvignon from Napa Valley and poured the wine for each of us. Mark looked directly into my eyes and said, "I am all yours, ask me anything, and go as deep as you wish. Now is the time."

So I began to ask him why he was so afraid to connect deeply with me, and he shared that he wasn't afraid. My intuition was telling me that I was accurate with this knowing, so I just smiled and listened to his rationale.

I began to see a pattern here that when you go through divorce and you haven't healed the pain, it follows you into all relationships, especially personal ones. I could feel the chemistry between us as we looked into each other's eyes. I thoroughly enjoyed this date with Mark. I love to dress up, have a nice glass of wine and deep conversation, and enjoy a delicious meal. Personal connection is so important to me as I feel it's a rare gift in this busy world. Mark's world was very busy on the outside, so these moments were rare and special. I offered to pay for half of the bill for supper, but he insisted and said, "Merry Christmas."

He was always a gentleman in all regard, and this I appreciated.

As we walked back to my vehicle holding hands, the snow was falling, and it was truly one of our best dates looking through my lens. He asked me to stay with him that night. I knew that he had a lot of drinks that night, so it would be a roll-over-and-go-to-sleep kind of night for us. I had bought him a nice bottle of scotch for Christmas, so he poured each of us a small glass to try, and then it was lights out.

I lay awake a lot that night, pondering the hamster wheel theory, where we have been programmed as a society to work to achieve the monetary things in life to bring us success and happiness. I could see that Mark was very successful in his career, and he openly would tell me that he was married to his career. That night I realized that this relationship was too slow for me. We had been dating for about four months, and I had only seen him about ten times. My counselor told me that taking it slow was a good thing in dating, but my intuition was telling me that this was not in alignment for me. I knew that I was going to have to talk to Mark about how I was feeling fairly soon.

The next morning I was tired from lying awake most of the night so I didn't feel like dealing with my thoughts at this time. He rolled over and pulled me close to him, kissing my shoulders and running his fingers along my naked back. I could feel the shivers running through my body as he caressed my skin. We had passionate morning sex. I knew inside that this would be the last time that we would be together sexually and most likely physically. We had a coffee together at the island overlooking the cold morning sunrise. I could tell that Mark wasn't feeling at the top of his game after the Christmas party last night. He told me that he was going to go into work for a bit. I wasn't surprised as that was his weekly routine. I packed up my bag, and he walked me down to my car. He opened my car door and gave me a kiss and said goodbye.

I was exhausted and truly needed to process all my thoughts. I really questioned myself as to why I drove through a whiteout snowstorm to pick up a man who was drunk. I was disappointed in my own lack of boundaries, but I vowed to myself in 2016, after my pulmonary embolism, that I was going to follow my heart and that I wouldn't be influenced by external opinions. I had no regrets, but I knew that this relationship wasn't in total alignment for my happiness.

The following day I sent a text to Mark and asked him if we could have a phone conversation. I opened up to him and told him that I needed more time with him as I wanted to truly dive in deep and see where this went. He once again told me that he was still deciding if this is what he wanted and needed more time. I agreed to do so.

This still didn't sit well with me. I thought to myself, *I am not going to sit in this internal confusion any longer.*

I decided to send him a text. In my message, I said that I wanted to go deeper into the relationship to see where it went and that I needed more. I was completely vulnerable with him. I had nothing to lose at this point. I wasn't going to settle for less.

He sent me text me back and told me that after careful consideration, he had to end our dating relationship because he just couldn't give it 100 percent and that he doesn't like to do anything that is not his full effort. I wasn't shocked, to be honest, as his actions had shown me that his job was his priority, and I could feel that he was afraid of commitment other than work!

I was hurt, but I also knew that it was for the best, and I truly enjoyed being treated like a woman from this attractive kind man. Mark was my sexy oil and gas executive who had fine taste in life. My conclusion was that many times the outside doesn't match the inside, because of external pressures of life. When you are caught up in the hamster wheel of life, you can sometimes lose internal balance and personal connection caused by external stress.

The downside of divorce for men is that they get caught up in the system of paying for their previous marriage, which leaves them little time for a new relationship. I have seen this several times, and it's hard to watch this imbalance affect everyone around them.

Mark and I ended on a good note. He sent me a text one night a few months down the road, asking how I was coping with COVID? We decided to connect via FaceTime one evening. It was nice to catch up and connect again. During the call, he said to me, "Why did we break up?"

I replied with, "Well, I am not sure."

He was having a rough day after a coworker had made comment referring to the point that Mark had no feelings so he would be okay. I said to him, "Well, actually, I can tell you some good things about yourself as I am writing your chapter right now."

He asked me if I was going to roast him. I said, "No, not at all."

I told him that he was an attractive man. He had a kind heart. He was charming, attractive, had beautiful eyes and a sexy smile. I also told him that he knew how to treat a lady with class. He then proceeded to tell me that I was a 10/10 for looks, that I was intelligent, and that I could back up my opinions, even if he didn't agree with me, and that was sexy as f&*k. He also told me that opposites attract and that he loved that I was a free spirit swimming with the whales in the ocean, that I was responsible, emotional, and a risk-taker. Then we laughed and said, "So why are we not dating?"

I always believe in ending all relationships with gratitude and kindness.

I know that I could always pick up the telephone and call Mark if I needed to, and that feels good to me. I know that our timing was off and that I was too deep for Mark's relationship needs. I am grateful for the four months that we spent together and that he showed me how a lady is to be treated. I will carry these values with me as a checkbox of what I want in future relationships.

I dive deep in all that I do. I am not a shallow dweller. Thank you, Mark.

CHAPTER 5

Hot Wife

Name: Tyler
Occupation: Pipefitter
Age: 45
Height: 5'11"

X-rated chapter!

Imagine an attractive woman who is married! You may call her a hot wife. That is exactly what I thought the definition was too when I was asked to be this on one of my first texting connections with Tyler! Well, let's just say that was *not* his definition of a "hot wife."

I will admit that being a forty-nine-year-old woman dating in the twentieth century has taught me a lot of how fast the world grows, and if you want to keep up, you need to learn quick. When I left my marriage of twenty-one years, I truly only went on two dates: one with a boyfriend Shane, whom I dated when I was twenty years old, and then Luke, whom I met on a dating app. My online dating expertise wasn't sharp at all when I began again in the fall of 2019.

There are so many new dating apps to choose from. You need a tutorial just to figure out how to write a profile on each different app and what all the new abbreviations mean. I have Googled many terms and abbreviations that I don't understand. I have educated myself very quickly to move from naïve to knowledgeable about a certain subject.

Tyler was one of the first men I had connected with on one of the newer dating apps. He was an attractive man who was fairly aggressive with his intentions for what he wanted from me. He began connecting with me, getting to know me in a fairly normal initial connection. Then once he felt that he knew me fairly well, he went in deep with his wishes. He knew exactly what he was looking for and wasn't going to stray from that need. He asked me if I would be willing to have sex with another man that we could choose together. This would include not using protection with that man so he could "clean" me up after the sexual act. I am not going to go into detail here about what that entails, but as you can imagine, I was in awe of this request.

He told me that he was insistent on how he would massage me before I would go and meet with another man and prepare me for our sexual connection. He then told me how he would worship my body after the act.

I felt naïve and completely out of touch with the new way of "dating." I quickly did some research to figure out what all the "*hotwiving*" involved. My first thought was, *What happened to you during your childhood that you think that this is normal?*

I understand being adventurous sexually, but this was beyond my perception or anything close to healthy for myself.

I quickly answered him with, "You will never groom me to want to take part in this scenario."

Being the healer/rescuer that I am, I have to admit that I did try to have a friendship with him to see what was underneath this thought pattern. But that quickly changed!

The other alarming thing that happened during our connection was he had tried to call me on FaceTime one morning unexpectedly. I naively called him back per his request. As we were connected visually, I could see his face and body. I suddenly began to realize that he was masturbating while he was talking to me on the phone. In my head, I was so shocked! I was thinking to myself that I need to hang up but was so shocked that I didn't follow through with my actions. I said to him, "What are you doing?" and he replied with, "I think you know what I am doing!"

I quickly replied with, "I have to go, and you shouldn't be doing that!"

After we had hung up, I sent him a text and said, "Don't ever do that again," as I felt so violated.

I truly began to understand the intentions behind men through my own experiences. When a man texts first thing in the morning and asks you for a photo, he is more than likely asking for a naked photo, and it's solely for the purpose of sexting and his masturbation needs. I caught onto this immediately and would actually call the man regarding his intent, and usually, he would admit that yes, he was only looking for a hook-up. This was *never* my style! It always shook me up as I truly began to ponder the fact that some women who lacked self-confidence may, in fact, go ahead with this request, thinking that down the road, it would turn into something more than just sex!

Tyler had ordered me a box full of lingerie and sex toys and had them delivered to my house. This was a first for me. The box said, "Goddess Velva Dawn" on it. I wondered why I hadn't blocked this man and just moved on. I knew that it was my big heart wanting to help him and figure out what childhood wound had occurred to have him want to carry out these actions with a woman.

I need to be very clear that I never ever met this man in person or had any intentions of doing so. He had tried for months for me to meet him for coffee, but I didn't feel safe in doing so.

The clarity that I received in this from him was he told me one day to put on a pair of high heels and to look at myself in the mirror and to see what other men see in me. I had never done this with lingerie on before as I was inhibited from lack of self-confidence having had three babies and my body changing over the years of being a mother and not putting myself first.

When you dive into the dating arena, self-confidence is key to have before you set up your profile. It will carry you a long way. If you aren't confident in how you look or feel, please do the deep work on your inner and physical body before you start looking for it externally. These are all the wrong reasons to seek that external validation. You will only attract the wrong, unhealthy relationship. I have tested this theory, trust me!

I always tell my married girlfriends that if you think that you are confident now, try dating where you have to relearn how to flirt again, keep your physical body in shape because you know that when you remove your clothes one day for a man in a relationship, that you want to be rock solid in your confidence regardless of size! Meeting for that initial connection takes courage, trust, and a leap of faith. It's like an interview each time you agree to meet on a first date. Over and over, you begin to build up confidence and to get crystal clarity on exactly what you are looking for, no exceptions. You learn the importance of maintaining your boundaries with your list of must-haves and holding out until you find that whole package that will compliment yours.

During one of my social gatherings with one of my friends, we began talking about our dating lives. She asked me whom I had been talking to recently on the dating apps. I was sharing with her about Tyler and how shocked I was by his requests. She said, "Please show me his photo as I am pretty sure that he connected with me also."

Bam! We had been contacted by him, and he had told us the same story. We talked about how shocked we were that a man had this request.

My gut feeling is that he has sent the invitation to many women to help him satisfy his sexual needs, and I will never know if any obliged, but I know that it certainly wasn't for me.

To each their own! I am not judging people for their sexual needs, but I know for certain what I feel comfortable doing and what I don't, and this was a *no*-go for me and always will be. Tyler brought something new into my life, and I learned from him. He gave me this awareness of how much the dating world has changed from 1989 and that I have so much to learn. The small-town girl who grew up on a farm near a hamlet in Alberta still had a lot of knowledge to gather to instill the "dating smarts" of 2020.

The platform that was inviting me to grow, learning who I was and what I wanted, had begun. I can see that if you were lacking confidence within yourself, you might easily be swayed. There are so many different people with unique needs out in the world, and when you are combining the dating world in this mesh, it can be complicated.

My best wisdom is to really have your own life figured out before you make a profile and put that online. Be honest with your intentions as to what you are looking for online. Are you ready for something casual, or are you seeking a long-term commitment?

Part of my intention for writing this book is to help educate people who are new to the dating apps learn the different options and intentions and to be mindful of what you are wanting and what can show up as possibilities in this search.

Hot wife is *not* for me, but I learned a valuable lesson with Tyler to keep my boundaries tight and that I am still a student of life!

CHAPTER 6

Bulletproof

Name: Hunter
Occupation: Investment property
Age: 52
Height: 6'1"

Projection, deflection, and the illusion of what's underneath that bulletproof vest!

As we know, men are often programmed to be the hunter-gatherer archetype, forging for their families and seeking protection if need be.

I met Hunter who had the most charming personality of any man I had been on date with up to this point.

We met on a dating app, and our common thread was my hometown, where I grew up. I was surprised when he had mentioned that he knew of the small town I grew up in was. He immediately asked if he could give me a call. I liked that he was willing to connect via phone immediately so we could hear each other's voices and get to talk on a deeper level than text.

Our first phone call, we talked for over three hours and had a lot in common. The second phone call that very same day was over five hours long. The conversation was fluid and easy, and we had a lot of laughter.

He was very honest with me during the conversation, stating that he had a past and that he wanted me to be okay with his past before we went any further in meeting each other. I did my own research on his past and always feel that until someone's actions have a negative effect on me, I will give him or her the benefit of the doubt. It's who I have always been and will continue to be; maybe it's the healer in me, I don't know, but I am proud of that characteristic. Now with that being said, it doesn't mean that I am naïve to life or will allow someone to walk all over me, but I am willing to give him or her a first chance with me.

We ended up agreeing to meet on our first date during the lockdown with COVID. We didn't have a lot of options to go out and meet, so I invited him over for a glass of wine one evening. I had my 911 girlfriends on call just in case I needed them. I know that my counselor is going to give me her opinion after she reads this as she has always said to me, "Dawn, please don't bring anyone into your home until you know them well."

During one of our conversations, he had asked me what my favorite color was, and I said purple. He showed up wearing a nice purple dress shirt on our first date. He came through the door and asked if he could have that shot of tequila that I had offered him over the phone as he was very nervous.

We laughed and had a shot of tequila while we decided what restaurant we were going to order food to be delivered from. His personality was joyous, and it lit up the room.

During the night, we talked a lot and had a lot of common goals when it came to personal growth, and he seemed open to my work and was very supportive of my goal of assisting others in their own personal empowerment. We decided to meet again shortly after for our second date.

We enjoyed many dates after this, cooking together, working out, and getting to know some mutual friends on either side. Finally, after a month, we agreed to delete our dating apps and to focus on our relationship.

My fiftieth birthday was coming up just over a month of our initial date. I wanted to plan a huge celebration with all my friends and family to celebrate this huge milestone, but of course, with the lockdown restriction of COVID, I couldn't have the celebration I wished to have. I decided to have a very small supper to enjoy another solar return.

As many who know me well know, I do enjoy sipping a good glass of tequila, so a Mexican restaurant was my choice for the evening. We all enjoyed our evening with the festive theme and a chance to visit with precautions.

The very next day, I began to feel very sick. In my gut, I knew that I had contracted COVID-19 as my lungs felt very heavy and my body didn't feel like anything that I had felt when I had been sick previously. I immediately booked a COVID test and had to wait a couple of days to get an appointment. Hunter also wasn't feeling good either and decided to come along for the ride as we were sick at this point, and so we could isolate together.

Upon receiving my results, I was, in fact, positive for COVID-19, the UK variant, which is exactly what my body was telling me. We spent a few days in bed sick together, mostly sleeping. He finally said, "I need to go home to sleep in my own bed."

My health began to deteriorate rapidly after my initial diagnosis, and I eventually ended in hospital on oxygen and steroids on the brink of having to go to ICU.

As I lay there during this illness, I kept in touch with Hunter, seeing how he has feeling, and vice versa. I had three moments during my illness where I was on the verge of dying and truly began to ponder what my priorities were in life and review all that I had accomplished up until this point at the age of fifty years old.

I had some very rough moments where the doctor came in and said that things aren't looking good and that I should let family know what's going on with me. It was like the virus had a mind of its own and took over my body. I felt as though I had no control over what would happen with this COVID infection. I surrendered to it all. I sent texts to few people who were very important to me and told them what was going on and that I was tired and that I didn't know if I could keep fighting anymore.

One person I trust deeply and have known for over thirty years, in particular, said something to me that truly resonated with my soul. I asked my soul if it was ready to go home, and I heard *no*. I wanted to stay and see my girls graduate from all their schooling, get married, and have children, if they chose to. I also had many more books to write and courses to create and that I truly hadn't even begun to live my fullest life yet.

I truly began to withdraw from everyone during this diagnosis, especially from Hunter. I knew that it was going to take some time for me to regain my health upon discharge from the hospital, so I had very little communication with him.

Finally, after not seeing each other for six weeks, he said to me, "Dawn are we done?"

I replied with, "Yes, I think so."

I just knew that I had to trust my gut feeling with all this and that what we had agreed to learn from each other felt complete at this moment and that I truly needed to focus on myself and my healing for months to come.

As I mentioned before, you can see that Hunter had a very vivacious personality, but what I saw underneath was an energetic bulletproof vest that he had put into place to protect himself from feeling too much. He is actually a very sensitive man and has endured a lot of pain in his life up until this point, which he tries to hide underneath so no one can see it, but I could.

You see, when someone comes across very strong and confident, sometimes underneath it all is an energy of being afraid of being vulnerable.

This relationship was one of a karmic oath in my perception and that we agreed to be there for each other during this very deep internal shift, and for this, I am grateful, and it felt complete.

Always remember to look below the bulletproof vest to see why it's been placed there in the first place. Some people come into our lives for a short time but have a very deep purpose as Hunter did for me.

CHAPTER 7

Return of the Exes

Circling Back

Be careful what you wish for!

Many times we often let our minds wander about our exes, whom we had dated in our past. Where are they now? What do they look like? What if we had stayed together? You have this natural curiosity to know what they are "up to" now. Now not all your old relationships are ones you are naturally curious about for sure, but some just make you go hmm.

I found out that quantum field is alive and kicking while writing this book. Each chapter drew in the invitation of reconnection with each person in each chapter. While writing this chapter, I had four ex-boyfriends contact me within two weeks. A coincidence? I think not, but a response to the energy that I was putting out into the universal flow. I believe that part of this was for unresolved healing on both sides of the coin. Being a teenager and dating, well, let's just say that one can be immature in how they treated another in the dating world.

I refer to the part in this book where I begin to ponder the learning of dating one person and marrying them for life comes from. In high school, it was a bit like this from my masculine programming. We were molded to date one "nice" boy. Of course, I chose the fast-tracked, fun, hard-loving bad boys to date in high school and still do for the most part. I seem to love the adrenaline rush, spontaneity, and the need to be different, a leader not a follower. I know many times that my parents would cringe at my choices in life, and it's a good thing that they don't know the half of what I did as a teenager, or they would have had a full head of gray hair years ago. I believe that some of us are born to light a fire in the world, blazing new trails for others to follow. It's all a choice; comforts versus conquer.

I have always felt comfortable having male relationships. In fact, I would say I feel more comfortable in the masculine relationships as I find that men are usually pretty black and white. They mean what they say; nothing more, nothing less, as my dad tells me. He said, "Women are always analyzing more than what a man says. Keep it simple."

I do believe that now that I am meeting different men and seeing that their intentions are pretty clear and simple. What you see is what you get.

I have always loved a man who can carry on the quick banter with me dishing it out as I can. There is something sexy about a man with a kind dry sense of humor and smart wit and a killer smile.

When I was married, I felt guilty about maintaining those male relationships in my life, so once I took my marriage vows, I ended most of my male relationships from high school. I was thankful for social media to be able to watch each of them grow into adults, having careers, families, and an adult life. I missed that male friendship and often wanted to just go for a coffee and catch up with many of them. Years passed and I began to ponder my loyalty to myself regarding this noncompliance to honoring male friendships in my life. I began to dig deeper into my own beliefs. Why did I feel that I couldn't have an innocent friendship with a male or even to dig even dipper into those roots of catching up with an ex-boyfriend? Why did I feel that it was so wrong to want to engage with an ex-boyfriend with the simple intention of finding out what they were up to thirty years later? Where did this come from? Is it engrained from society that once you were done in a previous relationship, they needed to be an ex for a lifetime? Was it jealousy from my husband at the time? Or was this my own issue? Or all the above?

As soon as I made the decision to retain a lawyer and proceed with our divorce, I felt free to reconnect with my old boyfriends and male friends from high school. One of my best supporters through the whole divorce was my high school friend Robert, who is a lawyer. He and I never dated in high school but hung out many times as good friends and kept in touch throughout our adult life, trying to meet a couple of times a year for supper to stay connected with our teenage community familiarity. He just knew when I needed a good talking to, keeping my intention focused on simply getting through the process of divorce, and when I needed to cry on the phone and have him just listen.

To this day, I am so grateful to be able to call him a good friend and to feel safe to share a tear, laughter, a good glass of red wine, or my latest dating scenario with him. He's truly a gift to me. It feels so free to be able to just be *me* and to have someone from your childhood town who knows your roots from way back grounding you into the now.

As we circle back to the ex-boyfriends, I want to talk about my first love Jax. Jax is that tall, dark-haired, handsome man who has the charming smile, dry sense of humor, and ultimate sex appeal. He was that guy whom all the girls who lived within a hundred miles of our small town wanted to date, and he knew it!

I was dating a "nice" boy who was also in the 4-H Beef Club with me, and we had many things in common: cattle, curling, music, and much more. I went to a party on the weekend, and Jax showed up. He asked if I would walk to the park and talk to him. I agreed to go and listen to what he had to say. He asked me if I would go out with him. I told him that I was already dating Mike and that I really liked him. He was pleading with me to take a chance on him.

I contemplated what Jax had said but really was into Mike and wanted to give our new relationship a fair chance. I decided to go to the local trade fair show in our small town and work as a volunteer at a booth for our 4-H Club. I could see Jax walking around the trade show with a few of my girlfriends. I was wondering what he was up to with his mischievous smile.

I was walking out of the booth to go home, and one of my girlfriend's walked up to me and asked me to go for a drive with her. I agreed. It wasn't just her in the car; Jax had made his way into the car and asked me again to go out with him and give him a chance. I thought to myself, *Wow, this guy is persistent, and I am definitely attracted to him.*

So I decided to give him a chance.

I broke it off with Mike, which was very hard for me to do being an empathic soul! I did feel guilty, but something was drawing me deeper to Jax. I was intrigued, and I wanted to see what he was all about.

Jax and I began dating and spent time together when we had time. He is a hardworking man and had at least two to three jobs after school, and I too had part-time job, looking after my 4-H steer and club activities, figure skating, and volleyball. We had a lot of fun together, and our dry sense of humor was a definite fit for sure. I felt at ease with him naturally.

I fell for this boy hard and fast. He had the tall-dark-and-handsome look with the sexy smile and charming words. I always felt like I had to worry about what girls were trying to pick him up as he had many eyes on him.

There was a graduation party in our neighboring town, and we went to the party. I knew that I had to leave the party as I had a curfew, and he didn't. I remember having a sick feeling in my stomach when I told him that I had to leave the party and he said that he was staying. I just knew that there was a good chance that he was going to cheat on me. It was my first real hit of my gut feeling inner knowing screaming at me to listen up. He pinky swore with me that he would be good and that he wouldn't cheat on me. As I drove away, I felt different.

The next morning my girlfriend called me and said, "Did you know that Jax cheated on you with a girl named Tiffany?"

My heart sank. That awful gut feeling was getting closer to being accurate. I called his house and asked him if I could come and talk to him. He did confirm that he had, in fact, cheated on me! My first heart-crush!

I thought to myself, *Well, you broke up with Mike to date Jax*, and then Jax breaks my heart just as I had broken Mike's heart; karma served on a silver platter—voila!

I pined over Jax for many months after we broke up. I have always believed that everything happens for a reason, and I didn't regret my decision. I was just left with a broken heart. Jax was the first man I gave my heart to, and that is a pretty special connection for a teenage girl.

I then met Jax's friend Alan. He was from a small neighboring town, and he drove a nice 1968 green Ford mustang with white leather seats. He seemed like a gentle soul on whom I could rebuild my trust in men again with the high school dating process.

After Jax broke my heart, I wasn't sure that I wanted to date anyone again as I was embarrassed from Jax cheating on me, which truly rocked my self-confidence. When someone cheats on you, it truly affects you on many different levels.

Alan knew this happened, and he treated my heart with tenderness and began to build my trust in men again. We dated for about five years from this point on. We clicked in so many ways and were great friends. When I graduated high school, he was going to remain living in the small town he was raised in, and I wanted to move to a bigger city to take my schooling and live in my first apartment away from my childhood home.

Eventually, we broke up when we realized that the big world had so many opportunities for us and we truly were too young to get married and settle down into married life. To this day, I keep in touch with Alan as he was a special man in my later high school years. I also keep in touch with Jax. We managed to mend fences, and he apologized for cheating on me back in high school.

I truly don't hold any grudges in life as I believe that everything happens for a reason and we grow more when we can forgive. There is always a lesson in experience on either side, but it's truly up to the individual to recognize that or not.

High school dating is the time when we are all emotionally maturing and having fun. Marriage seems so stressful compared to those days; less responsibility, I suppose, more courage and a zest for life.

Remember that when people circle back into your life, there may be some karma to clear and some unresolved lessons. Look at it like it's the universe delivering an option to level-up your perception. You will either keep circling within the same loop, or you will spiral up into a new experience and an expanded view of life with the same people.

I believe that we connect with a certain group of souls on the planet to learn our lessons from. If you review those certain people, they probably feel like family to you, and/or you can't get them out of your mind, which can mean that you are energetically deeply connected in this lifetime. Don't be afraid to follow those strings of healing and see the gift in what that exchange may offer you.

I am a person who has many friends from elementary school, high school, college, etc. When I connect with someone, I treasure that connection and put a concerted effort into maintaining those relationships.

Dating Mike, Jax, and Alan in high school gave me lessons of the heart and a barometer for what I was looking for when I got married.

Don't fear the circle-backs! They all come with a lesson, which is a gift.

CHAPTER 8

Cougar Love

Name: Coleman
Occupation: Accountant
Age: 32
Height: 6'4"

I had always wondered what it would feel like to be called a cougar!

I truly believe that your energy shows your age. I had always dated men older than myself previous to my marriage. It was a learned behavior from watching those around me that the woman was younger than the man.

As I put up my profile on the dating apps, I was able to choose my age range in the men I was seeking a potential relationship with. My age range was forty-three to forty-nine at the time. Now of course, there were those who slid under and over the range.

This was the time in my life to really question, does age matter to me? Was I willing to look beyond the old-school programming I had in place? Wouldn't it be a benefit to date a younger man with more energy? I was certainly open to letting go of my old masculine perceptions of what I thought a relationship should look like.

Coleman was one of the men to begin to invite me into that space of questioning that scenario within myself. He sent me a message on one of the apps, asking me about myself. When I saw that he was thirty-two years old, I immediately wanted to delete the message because of his age. I then began questioning myself about age and what is its significance to me in a relationship. He was a very well-educated man, being an accountant, and was respectful toward our messages.

I asked him why he would be interested in an older woman, and he said age didn't really matter to him and that he liked women who are older because they are mature and they know what they want, usually! I agreed with him and decided to begin to unravel this old belief system within myself. He was a good-looking man, and we had good communication so far.

Over the months, we continued talking, and I continued to let go of control of those rigid belief systems.

Coleman was planning a drive to meet me as he was from a town a couple of hours from me. The timing didn't work out for us to meet, and I eventually knew that it wasn't meant for us to meet, but I was grateful for the beginning of this unraveling.

Then I met this amazing man, Dan, who was nine years younger than myself. He had eyes that lit up the room and a smile that would melt your heart. He was a hardworking, old-fashioned type of man. He reminded me of my grandfather, Dave Silver, in so many ways. He loved to be outdoors, he was comfortable with animals, and he would open the truck door for me each and every time.

I had some very deep talks with Dan about how I was older than him and if he felt that our age difference would have an impact down the road. He firmly told me that age doesn't matter to him. He said that he was attracted to me and that we had similar interests, so that was the key.

He didn't have any children, which, being a mother, I know that value of having children, if you have that wish inside of you. Now I am way beyond my pregnancy days. In fact, we had our three girls early on so we could retire early and travel. But that part of my life, having a baby, truly was over. I brought this up to him and asked him how he felt about not having children. He told me that his two dogs were his children, and he had nieces and nephews to fill that void. That made sense to me.

As we continued to see each other over the months, he began to withdraw back into his shell of wanting to be alone more often. He is a very hard worker, running his own construction business and doing other jobs on the side.

When he began to withdraw from me, I asked him what was going on inside of his head. He said, "I feel like I am depressed."

He asked me to give him some time to sort it out. I was beginning to wonder if he had a fear of being vulnerable and commitment. I too have had to work through these exact same emotions constantly, but I am lucky to have the tools to do so. Many people don't have the emotional tools to deal with these feelings when they come up, and they can be ashamed to ask for help. This can tie back into the old masculine archetype, where the man is strong and is the provider and shows no emotions.

After a few weeks of Dan withdrawing, I felt it was best if we were just friends as I didn't feel that he was truly ready for a deep committed relationship, and I certainly wanted something deeper than casual.

To this day, Dan and I are still friends, and I hope that we always will be. He helped me work through my issues of being a cougar with a younger man.

In my experience, when you are shining with your own power and light, many souls will feel your frequency and want to connect with you. He or she may not be aware as to why they are attracted you, but the main point is that they can feel your light. Age is truly an old archetypal system that was put into place to get married, have a family, and grow your roots. What matters most is your connection to another person!

The clearer your core gets, the faster your frequency will vibrate. I don't hide my photos or my thoughts anymore from social media. The best tool when someone becomes abusive, overstepping his or her boundaries on social media, is to block them. Healthy boundaries are key to holding your own power. The days of hiding your body and dimming your light are on their way out.

You will find the clearer your energy becomes, the younger you will look! The happier you are, the more peaceful your life will be. Your physical body shows the wear and tear that your heart goes through. It's time to redirect that love to your inner self and then watch the mirror reflect, through your own lens, your inner truth.

CHAPTER 9

Beautiful Stranger

Name: Blake
Age: 43
Occupation: Oil and gas business owner
Height: 5'10"

Hello, beautiful stranger!

Every woman can appreciate a man who takes care of his body, is sensual, kind, caring, takes control, and ignites that sexual energy within her soul. Meet Blake! I call this man my beautiful stranger because the moment he connected with me on the one dating app, I knew this was pure sexual chemistry and that it would be fast and furious. Envision this man with beautiful blue eyes, sandy blond hair, and a smile that will melt your heart, a body with strong sleeve-tattooed arms, sculpted legs, and a beautiful ass.

When he sent me a message the first time, I looked through his profile photos, and I could feel his warm energy. I knew instantly that he was going to be in my life to teach me a powerful lesson. I felt that our connection sexually would be short but hot and connected. I knew that I wasn't going to deny myself this connection, regardless of what my girlfriends were telling me that they thought of him. You see, I would always show my girlfriends a potential date's dating profile to get a second and third opinion before moving on to meeting them in person.

When my friend Patti saw his profile photos, she said to me, "Dawn, he looks like a player, you should stay away from that scenario as you will get hurt."

I replied with a quote that I saw, and it says, "I heard that you are a player, nice to meet you. I am the coach."

As I am sorting through the labels of the dating world, I am truly trying to disassemble these labels and follow through with what my soul needs to learn.

Now I have dated "players" in the past as I tend to be attracted to the bad boys with their strong masculine sexual auras. Blake and I had exchanged messages for about three to four weeks before we agreed to meet on our first date. We had decided to keep it simple with a bottle of wine and conversation to see how it flowed. As soon as he walked through my front door, with a nice bottle of red wine and his smile, I knew that he was going to be trouble in my bedroom.

Conversation flowed easily with him. He has a very soft kind nature to him and that strong sexual masculine energy that wants to take control of you in the bedroom kind of duality. We had some wine and continued deepening out personal connection through conversation. I could feel the sexual chemistry between us as we stood close to each other. We had decided to order some food in and continue with the easy conversation.

I had to admit that I was admiring his sexy, strong, sleeve-tattooed arms and icy blue eyes. I had never dated a man with tattoos before, so this was an interesting find for me. I have two tattoos of my own, so I was definitely not against anyone having them. I just hadn't dated a man with them. I was very intrigued by Blake. He seemed open-minded, which I admired and amplified his sexy status. He was asking me questions about my work, my book, etc. He has three children of his own and is a very successful business owner in the oil and gas industry. He has been divorced for quite a few years and has been in the dating world a bit longer than I had. He was easy to talk to, and I felt as though I could ask him anything that I was wondering.

I decided to wear my tight leather-like material pants and a black halter-style top. I had sprayed my most sensual perfume in my hair, on my body, to fit the energy of the evening. I felt good about my body as I have been taking good care of my physical and spiritual body for many years. I have to admit that I was a bit intimidated by the fact that Blake was five years younger than I was and had the body of a sexual god in my eyes, but I was excited to see where this connection would lead to.

I told myself that I was going to follow that soul-calling and listen to my internal self, so this was one of those times when I was pacing the floor yet again, talking to my girlfriend Patti about why I put myself through these nervous moments in my life. Dating isn't for the faint of heart as it takes a lot of vulnerability and courage to put yourself out there, especially when you are dating a hot younger man.

As Blake and I stood beside each other near the island, sipping our wine, he took his hands and held my face, gently kissing me with his full lips. He was a sensual kisser. He slid his hands around my waist and pulled me into him. I could feel his tight body against mine, and the sexual chemistry was running high between our two bodies. We slowly made our way to the bedroom. Everything with Blake felt natural and easy, so my nerves had calmed down, and I was looking forward to the next stage of our evening.

We had already had the safe-sex talk, which also put my mind at ease as his, I am sure. He was very seductive in how he slowly took off my clothing, kissing me, and using his hands to explore every part of my body along the process of embracing each other's naked bodies. I was telling my girlfriends that I couldn't wait to run my hands across his naked body and feel the love that he puts into his physical body daily. They all giggled at me and agreed. I felt like a kid in a candy store with Blake.

Here I was, this forty-eight-year-old mother of three with this sexy hot younger man in my bed. Yes, I was nervous, but the excitement took over that nervous energy within minutes. I had imagined that Blake would be an experienced lover, and that he was! I had brought up some coconut tequila for each of us to slowly drip onto each other's bodies. He told me that this was a new experience for him, but he was excited to try it. He was a gentleman in the bedroom, being very considerate and always asking before taking any action. His lips caressed every part of my body. I could feel this intense fire light up inside my soul as our energies collided. He was fulfilling one of my bucket-list items of having sex with a younger man, but at the same time, I was fighting my ego, telling me that he might run when he saw my body naked.

I allowed myself to truly surrender and just be in the moment with Blake. His demeanor was very seductive yet gentle and calm. He took control in the bedroom with respect and compassion. He moved me in positions that were new to me but felt so good. I fully trusted him, and the coconut tequila and the glass of red wine helped calm any worries that I may have had.

I enjoyed every ounce of his body and soul during this time together. We had talked previously about each other's needs and wants so we had an idea of how to get there before we physically did. He was an amazing lover. My body felt so much pleasure from head to toe as our bodies were entangled in sexual lust for hours. I kept thinking to myself every older woman should have a sexual experience with a younger man who is hot and knows his way around a woman's body like Blake does. We laid in bed and began to watch a movie together before he drove home.

That night all I could think about was the endorphins that were running through my body from the hours before. The sex was more than I had expected in a very amazing way. He had truly taken any sexual experience that I had had previously to a whole new level. I had truly gone into this connection with Blake for a hook-up to move through some of my own fears of being the older woman, etc. Sexually, we were very, quite compatible, and that night I was already thinking of when we could connect again.

My girlfriends all asked me how the "date" went. I just smirked and said that every woman should experience a night like that with a man like Blake! Many of my girlfriends are always telling me that they are living vicariously through me. I am actually living the life of following my soul and releasing the old labels that we have created in this cultural paradigm that we have now outgrown.

Blake is truly a positive, amazing man. He would text me in the morning, greeting me with either, "Hello, sunshine" or "Good morning, babes." When you receive a warm greeting like that, it warms the soul and opens the connection between two people.

We continued talking, texting, and connecting over the next few weeks sporadically when we could connect between his parenting schedule and mine. He worked in the city, periodically having business meetings, so he had planned to stop by on his way through a few times. We continued to talk openly about how each of us felt and what we had wanted in this connection.

I was very open with him and told him that I wasn't looking for a serious commitment as I had just broken off an engagement in an unhealthy relationship previous to this, so I wanted to keep it light and easy. He agreed with me and said the same about himself. I knew that we wouldn't have a long time together but was enjoying it in the moment. You see, I was truly and still am learning to live in the present moment versus trying to figure out the end. This isn't an easy thing to do.

One Sunday he invited me to come out to his acreage and have a glass of wine and a visit. I was happy to go for a drive and venture out to his part of the world. As I drove out to his place, I enjoyed the drive as my aunt and uncle had once lived out near his place, so I had a lot of déjà vu along the drive. I was raised on a farm, so I wasn't afraid of long drives in the country solo.

As he greeted me at the door with a warm smile on his face in his boxer shorts and a T-shirt, I was very impressed with his sexy greeting. He poured each of us a glass of wine, had the music playing, and we sat on his bed, reconnecting and talking. I was very attracted to Blake, and the sexual chemistry was very strong between us, so it didn't take long for us to be naked in his bed, exploring each other's bodies with passion and respect. I admired how he treated me like a lady, always thinking of me during our interactions. We jumped into the shower during the afternoon, and he even held my hair so it didn't get wet. He knows how to treat a woman, which I deeply respected.

I always felt that I had known Blake before in another lifetime and that we had come together in this lifetime to heal the past karma between our souls through this deep sexual connection, friendship, and trust. I had always known that we wouldn't be together in a committed relationship but that we will always be good friends once the sexual relationship was done, and that is exactly what happened.

I gained so much in the short few months of our sexual connection, but to this day, we will still remain good friends. Don't get me wrong my door is always open for Blake sexually, if neither one of us is in a relationship, but I do respect that man with a deep underlying knowing that he feels the same for me. We knew that it was time for that part of our connection to be over, but we still keep in touch, asking each other how our lives are going, etc. I appreciate the mature honesty, clear communication, and respect that we have for each other. There was no ghosting in our ending but a true authentic knowing that we were willing to be vulnerable about. He taught me that a beautiful stranger could touch my soul through a deep past-life connection, and that was all that was needed in our sacred exchange. My wish is that every woman can have an experience like I did with Blake once in her lifetime to feel the deep passion between two souls with no strings attached but with a very deep respect and friendship.

Thank you, Blake, for helping me unwind the sexual goddess within me.

CHAPTER 10

Instant Chemistry

Name: Brett
Age: 46
Occupation: Business owner
Height: 5'11"

Do you remember when you were a child, and you touched something hot for the first time? A stove, an iron, or a curling iron? It may have been the first connection to your inner senses to that nervous system that forewarns you of something dangerous.

This is similar to the system that I use when I meet someone on the first date. Being an intuitive empath, I can feel immediately if there is any chemistry with this person and also if they have worked through a lot of energy in their pain body. Sometimes I can be blindsided if I am not taking care of myself and am leaning toward the "settle" side of what I am wanting.

Years ago, my counselor had me do a chart for my dating life that had "what I need" on one side, "what I can allow to slide" in the middle, and "what is not acceptable" on the right side. It was one of the best charts that I have ever created as it allowed me to dive deep into myself and think about what I truly wanted in a romantic partner, not what landed at my feet. I had a friend say to me the other day, "Dawn, you really did a spreadsheet on what you want in a relationship? Doesn't that take the magic out of it?"

I responded with, "Well, when you put your intentions out to the universe, then you have given the universe your personal equation with clarity, which will help get the sum of that equation."

He said, "Well, my dating life isn't going so well, so send me the steps to make that chart!"

I do believe that when you take the time in stillness to intend what you need in a romantic relationship, the quantum field will send that vibration out, inviting that similar or more expanded vibration back into your life. I have been working with this frequency for quite some time now and can feel it within a few minutes of meeting someone new.

Instant chemistry is the best science experiment one can ask for. Now I have been on many first dates. One week I had one date per day. I wanted to accomplish a few things in doing so. First, it is a self-confidence builder. When you drive up to meet a total stranger in a new location, this takes courage and vulnerability. I wanted to do this to see how I handled it. The second thing that I wanted to accomplish was to see if I felt instant chemistry with each man.

I remember one time driving up to the agreed location and thinking that the man I was meeting was standing outside the restaurant, and if this was him, I thought, I am not doing this date. I wasn't attracted physically to this man at all. I was talking to my girlfriend Patti on the phone, and she said to me, "Just drive away. He will never know it was you!"

I knew that I couldn't just drive away as I have my old honest roots instilled in me, and I had to at least suffer through a coffee with him. So I parked my vehicle and was mentally preparing myself to get through the next thirty minutes with this man or whom I thought was this man.

As I got out of my vehicle, a tall handsome man popped his head out of a car that was already parked and said, "Hello, Dawn!"

He was tall, handsome, and had great energy. I actually laughed out loud and said, "Oh, aren't you a surprise!"

We spent the next four hours in deep conversation, enjoying each other! The first date is much like a business interview as you each ask questions that are important to you, listening to the answers and watching for any red flags.

During our conversation, a huge red flag appeared for me: He had never been married or had been in a long-term committed relationship. He was also going to be moving soon and had no children. I have found that men who have not been in a committed relationship may have some fear of commitment and usually aren't stable in a relationship. I also prefer men who have had children as they usually carry a deeper compassion for life and understand responsibility to another level.

Back to my point about instant chemistry, I believe, for myself, it's either there upon arrival or not. It's like when the quantum field has been programmed with your intentions, and then you connect with the other person's vibration, you "know" instantly if there is a connection. I believe we have been programmed from society's old belief systems through the foundations of religion that we need to "make" things work, even though they may not feel in alignment naturally, i.e., arranged marriages could possibility fit into this category.

Our auras talk to one another when we are far apart, when we are truly connected to another person. If that instant chemistry isn't there, then I find it hard to open up and be vulnerable to that person. There is an instant shield that I feel, which is truly my signal that I need to honor these boundaries from Mother Nature and move on, releasing my own fear of hurting another's feelings because I don't feel the chemistry.

I have seen the "ghosting" affect in the dating world and have done it myself, when one simply doesn't have the courage or confidence to tell the other person that they just don't feel the chemistry. You silently hope that the other person picks up on your avoidance of their text messages and/or phone calls and disappears to never be seen or heard from again! This is an easy pattern to fall into, but we must remember that the energetic footprint follows us down the road into the future. The same lessons appear in different people until we consciously make the choice to look at the lesson head on and face it. Instilling healthy boundaries for yourself can be difficult if you have abandonment issues and a soft heart but are key for your energetic health and others.

When you realize that the quantum field is responding to your intentions and choices, you will soon begin to make choices that are for your highest good—period. If you see this string of avoidant people in your life, it could be a direct result of your own actions. Have you been avoiding ending relationships? Have you been keeping people hanging in the ethers of your circle just to have someone and not be alone? I always say choose quality over quantity in any area of my life, and dating is no exception to me.

Chemistry is the first key to opening the possibility of an intimate relationship with another through my lens. I have tried to skip that key and hope and pray that it will just magically grow with the other qualities that I see fitting in a possible relationship. Energy doesn't lie. When you feel that dense vibration in front of you, it's hard to move through it, under it, or around it. It's simply just not there. Many times we try to force things to happen because we see a few areas that are possible fits. When you think that, if you try to fit the wrong key into the keyhole of a door, it doesn't matter how many ways you turn the key; it simply won't fit. There is one direct configuration that is in alignment and will unlock the feminine and masculine energy to the doorway of the step. Sometimes we get stuck in trying to force the key into the opening when if we just could take a step back and see it as a strong signal from the universe that it's just not a fit—period. Don't try to overanalyze it or dissect what you did wrong or project blame. Simply leave the door locked, hold the gratitude from the lesson at the door, and continue sitting in the wholeness of the programmed quantum field that you have created to attract the unique key just for *you*.

To me, chemistry is when I can feel the person in front of me open, alive, and vulnerable. When I can feel my heart opening, all my senses are activated, radiating out into my quantum field like feelers wanting to know more. My heart beats faster, I can feel an excitement in my stomach. He smells good to me, I want him to be closer to my physical body and to feel drawn into his quantum field naturally. This is the beginning of instant chemistry for me!

If this is missing, then I know now to move on, being honest with other person and trust that I am honoring myself and the programming in my quantum field to guide me into the perfect alignment where the key will naturally open the right door. No need to get a new lock, but recognize that it's not the right fit.

The universe is pretty simple when you are in the flow of life. As humans, we tend to overanalyze and make it way more complicated that it is intended to be.

CHAPTER 11

Word Salad

Name: Romeo
Age: 45
Occupation: Salesperson
Height: 5'11"

Wherefore art thou, Romeo?

Last-ditch effort before quitting the dating apps! I decided to try one last dating app as a few of my friends had told me that they had success on this one app. I find this dark, handsome man with a beautiful smile and a dimple in his chin. His photo screamed trouble mixed with a load of speed, but I sent off a salutation when we were matched.

Now rewind a few months before this connection with Romeo. I went on a date with another man named Travis. This date was met with a beautiful white smile and a jacked-up black truck. Yes, you can imagine what was going through my head when I saw this. He laughed when he walked up to me and said, "Yes, that truck is ridiculous, I know."

I didn't say a word but smiled and thought to myself, *Is this the beginning of the unraveling of a huge ego?*

Conversation flowed easily with Travis. He was a successful CEO of his own self-made company. The second date felt more like a business interview to be honest. He was asking me questions about if my work could be done from anywhere as he likes to close his seasonal business down and travel for a few months of the year.

I have learned to watch to see if your actions align with your words. Are you feeding the word salad inviting me into your turmoil of shattered thoughts and intentions? Time and patience always equal clarity in all relationships from my experience.

Now let's talk about Romeo. I have been in the dating game for approximately eighteen months and after the instant-chemistry/ghosting sequence, I was ready to pull the pin on all apps and shut down the dating for some time. One of my friends said, "Have you tried this new social media dating app that is free?"

I replied, "No, I haven't tried that one."

So I thought to myself, *Let's give this one app one last try before pulling the pin and taking a sabbatical.*

As I was scrolling through, I saw this handsome chiseled face with a wicked smile. It said that this man lived closed my hometown. We were a match, so I sent off a message that said something corny like, "Romeo, if I had seen your handsome face around town, I would have remembered it."

He replied with, "Velva from Okotoks, how are you?"

We corresponded through text for a bit, and then he asked me to come to his house as he was going to make me supper. Per usual, I have my girlfriends on close 911. I can call in case I feel unsafe or if I need a rescue remedy moment to get me out of the hot seat. I always believe in safety first when it comes to meeting men online on first dates.

As I was driving the seventeen minutes from my house to his house, I was really reviewing in my mind if I was up for the continued adventure of dating. It takes a lot of time to get to know someone each time you begin a relationship. So over and over, this experience can be monotonous, and I didn't want to treat this date with an unconscious connection. The effort needed to be conscious from both parties.

As I rang his doorbell, he answered with door with a beautiful smile. I could smell the chicken cooking in the oven and see that he had went through quite the effort to prepare this supper for me with a clean apartment, candles were lit, soft music was playing, and he had a bottle of red wine open on the counter with two glasses.

My immediate response was that the effort was there on his end, so I needed to match his exchange and open up to the initial supper date. We enjoyed casual conversation getting to know each other over an amazing home-cooked supper. I did notice one red flag during supper, him name-dropping, which made me perk up and pay attention as to why he was name-dropping who he had dated in the past on our first date.

We were definitely physically attracted to each other. He was a very energetic person, always planning ahead and making goals, which is something that was on my list.

He asked me on the second date at the end of our first date, which is always a good sign that there is mutual interest in each other. I was impressed that he made the effort to cook me dinner.

As he walked me down the stairs to my car, we stopped, and he leaned in and kissed me.

Over the next few weeks, he came on strong. He asked if he could go hiking with my brother, and I was hesitant as I don't introduce the men I am dating to my family unless it's serious. I agreed to allow Romeo to join us on our hike. Now this was our third date. I was a nervous wreck as I exercise but to go hiking with a man on a third date was a bit out of my comfort zone to spend that much time with some and then have the double connection of my brother joining us.

We left in the wee hours of the morning, around five o'clock, to be at the base of the hiking trail by 6:00 a.m. He arrived on time with two shakes that he had made for us. We packed our gear and were off.

We met my brother in the dark in the parking lot. When I saw Romeo pack his laptop in his backpack, I thought to myself, *What are you going to do with that on a hike?*

My brother saw this too and without hesitation said, "What are you doing with a laptop on a hike?"

Romeo replied with, "Well, I don't want to miss a sale!"

Glen looked at me, and we read each other's minds that this is a red flag waving in the sky.

Would I recommend a strenuous hike on your third date? Probably not. Romeo asked me if I wanted to take a selfie with him, and I could feel this energy of escapism rising within my body. I know that I have a fear of being vulnerable in relationships, and it was clearly showing up with this date.

After the hike, we went to a local pub for a bite to eat with my brother. I overhead Romeo telling my brother that a good woman is hard to find, using online dating, and that as soon as he found me, he went off all the dating apps as he doesn't like using them in the first place. I literally held my breath and left the table to use the washroom. My gut was screaming at me that this guy was moving way too fast, and my inner knowing was exploding with the thoughts of be careful with this one.

He had to go back to work for a bit when we were done with our hike. I had ordered some sushi for us, and he picked it up on his way back to my house. We sat and talked about the day. I brought up what he had said to my brother about the online dating, and he said that he went off the apps.

I discussed with him that I hadn't as of yet as this was only our third date. Now when I am dating someone on more than a second date, I don't date other men. I feel it's not fair to either of us if our energy is diverted. I feel that to give someone a fair chance, you need to give them all your dating attention, just the way that I do things.

A few months went by, and Christmas was approaching fast. I found that Romeo came on fast and wanted to be together a lot. He was staying at my house six out of seven nights. I felt as though I needed my space. I also knew that when someone is coming on this fast, it could be a sign of an anxious codependent need in a relationship. It felt draining sometimes, and I was mindful to not repeat old patterns that I had in my marriage.

We hadn't been dating for a long time, so I was going to get him some simple gifts for Christmas, and we had decided to cook the meal together. He had wanted to invite his friend, which I was totally okay with, but her plans had changed, and she didn't join us.

I enjoyed cooking with him. Then it came time to open our gifts, and I could feel myself getting anxious as I am working on receiving from others. He had three gifts nicely wrapped in separate boxes. I had decided to gift him many smaller gifts and a canvas of him on the beach, which was one of his favorite photos.

As I began to open my gifts, he had bought me some very thoughtful gifts, which he knew I would like and could use when I went hiking. It seemed a bit excessive to me as we had only known each other for few months, but I was grateful.

I am always mindful not to introduce any man I am dating to my daughters unless it feels like it's going to move to the next level for me. I keep my dating life separate from being a mom and from my work. Healthy boundaries are key.

Romeo had never met my daughters as I didn't feel right about this. We planned to have another couple over to celebrate New Year's Eve. We had a fun night playing cards and games and enjoying appetizers. We were playing this one game, and the card said, "Cheers your glass if you are in a serious relationship," and I didn't raise my glass, but Romeo did. Once again, I could feel the confusion going on inside my head as it all felt too fast.

A few weeks after New Year's, he began to distance himself, saying he had work plans or had to go to the mall to go shopping. One of my girlfriends called me and said, "Hey, are you still dating that man?"

I replied with, "Yes, why do you ask?"

She said, "I am pretty sure that I saw his profile on a dating app?"

Once again, I was validated by that inner feeling of something being off. I immediately created an account for this dating app as it was one that I hadn't been on before. Sure enough, there he was, and the account showed that he was recently on the app within twenty-four hours.

Second time around this had happened for me when a man lied to me about going off a dating app and continued to window shop for other women. I was hurt and angry. Romeo told me that he was driving to another city to visit one of his male friends and that he was staying overnight! I started to put two and two together and realized that he was cheating on me with another woman, and I needed to find proof.

I called him while he was driving, and I confronted him about finding his profile on the dating app, and he immediately denied it and told me that it was an old account. I said, "The app shows that you were recently on it within twenty-four hours."

He got angry and started projecting onto me.

I took a breather and really thought this all over. Now it was all making sense to me, those feelings of confusion and being smothered. I felt angry that I let him push his way into my hike with my brother and Christmas and New Year's. I felt taken advantage of in many ways.

We talked through this and said that we would remain friends. He told me that he had feelings for me as I did for him after the months of dating and sharing.

I would always send him a text good night as he would to me. I went away for a weekend with a group of girlfriends to celebrate her fiftieth birthday. Romeo agreed to watch my dog for me. He was good with animals and was happy to watch her for me. He was snapping me photos of himself with my dog and said he enjoyed her company. I appreciated his help as I knew that she was in good hands. We talked on the phone for my long drive home from my weekend getaway. He told me that he would bring my dog back to my house as he was going to a football party with a group of men he worked with.

When I arrived home, my dog was safe and sound. I sent him a text to thank him and asked if he still had her medication as I couldn't find it in the house. He said, "Oh yes, I forgot it, sorry."

I said, "Well, I need it for morning," so he said that he would drive it over to my house and spend the night.

I truly enjoyed the fact that he would hold me in his strong arms each night, which was a secure feeling as I slept feeling his body next to mine.

I still had feelings for this man, which I was trying to move to the side, as I knew that he was long gone out of the relationship a while back from his presence on the dating app. I was smart enough to know that when a man lies about being on a dating app, it's truth that he is.

A few nights later, I sent him a text good night. He had asked if he could borrow my gas generator to vacuum out his camper as he wanted to go camping the following weekend. He had asked me if I wanted to join him for a bonfire if he went, and I agreed to do so. We had plans of doing the West Coast trail hike also, even though we weren't dating.

The morning after I sent the text, I received a message from a woman I wasn't friends with on social media. She began asking me in a message how I knew Romeo. I responded with, "Well, we were dating for a few months, but now we are in a different space of being friends with sporadic sexual connections."

She asked me if she could call me as she had something to tell me.

I instantly knew what it was. She told me that he had been on her couch for the last week. Now he had told me that he was taking a week off work and was driving out to BC to visit a friend for a week. I even sent him a text to ask him how his trip was going, and he lied and said that it was good. This woman then came over to my house, and we had coffee. She told me that she had a feeling that something was off with him as he was coming on really strong with her. She noticed the evening that I sent him a text to say good night that his phone lit up the bedroom. She said that she sneaked over when he was sleeping to see who was sending him a text at 11:00 p.m. She saw my name and then knew that she needed to contact me to ask more questions.

He had asked her to go camping with him and had told her that he had borrowed a friend's generator to vacuum out his camper. I said, "Yes, that was my generator!"

He had also sent her photos of my dog and told her that he was watching a couple's dog while they were out of town, and to top off the story, she then confided in me that he had taken her on their first date right before he showed up to spend the night with me. Bam! He was caught in his own tracks.

I called him and asked him to bring back my generator. He agreed and showed up within a few hours with my generator in his hand. As he was walking out of my garage I asked him when he was going to tell me that he had a girlfriend. He replied, "I don't have a girlfriend."

I said, "Oh really, well, I had a woman named Carol call me this morning, asking how I knew you, and she told me that you have been parked on her couch all week and that you didn't go to BC to visit your friend!"

He was shocked.

I said, "Why do you have to hurt people with your cheating actions?"

He was angry and told me that he had to call her and explain. Needless to say we were done with the word salad that Romeo was spinning from his lips.

My lesson from this relationship was that if your gut is telling you something, then listen to it! When a man is coming on strong and fast, it's not a healthy way to build a foundation for a long-term relationship. If you find him on a dating app, call it quits as he's just not that into you!

CHAPTER 12

Reflections from a Goddess

The Gift of the Unwinding

Reflections from the unwinding of my own masculine.

I truly believe that collectively, we are unwinding the patriarchal energy of the systemic programming that once fit our society for our needs and values. Life has a natural cycle of death and rebirth for all things. What we truly need to learn to do better is to release what is no longer working without attachments. It's truly a time of simplifying life and getting to the root of what is important to remain balanced.

As we see these patriarchal systems unwinding around us, it is also happening within us. Every living energy has a feminine and a masculine energy within to procreate energy. Every woman, man, and child has a feminine and a masculine energy within. The feminine energy in a natural state is very nurturing, open to receiving, heart-based, and all-knowing. The masculine energy is your action energy, your goal-setting ability, your strength, and your giving ability. When these two energies are in stasis, you will feel a natural state of peace. In the meantime, collectively, we have been working to level up the feminine and masculine systems for many years. We go through rebirth and evolve, and then the old systems die off, and we begin again.

The unwinding of the masculine within myself began when I knew I needed to leave my marriage. Unwinding the belief that one needs to be married for an entire lifetime was a big unwinding for me. I could feel deep in my soul that our connection in this lifetime was over, but then I had to work my way through the programmed feelings of guilt, shame, anger, disappointment, the loss of a dream, fear, and the huge discomfort of the unknowing of what was next. It took a lot of courage to follow my heart. It took me about five years to move through it, enough to be able to accept that I deserved to be happy and to create new dreams again. Leaving a long-term relationship and/or marriage takes time to move through the grief cycle into acceptance.

If I could go back now, I would have waited to begin dating a few years after my divorce, but I am an Aries, and I can be stubborn. So I tend to jump into the middle of the fire and then wonder how I am going to get out. I am a true believer that everything happens for a reason. We truly fail forward in life, and this is where we gather the most wisdom is in these times of messy change.

Each man I have met in the dating process helped me see that areas of the masculine within myself that I still needed to heal. I believe that when another person triggers you, it's a sign of an unhealed part of yourself that needs work. I also believe that every man who came into my life was to help me unwind the old masculine beliefs that I collected through the lens of my childhood up until this very moment. We gather and implement these beliefs until we outgrow them. For some, it's a lifetime, and for others, you move through the unwinding rapidly as your soul knows exactly the universal pace that you are ready for.

My work began in 2009 with the divine feminine. In 2012, I published my first book *Ancient Secrets of the Goddesses* and created the Goddess Healing Matrix™ System. I was then guided to write this book called *Unwinding the Divine Masculine* and have created an educational component to support the masculine unwinding within each of us. My goal is to learn to continue living an internal balanced energy, which will reflect externally. Life is truly an inside job. The internal work that we do is a direct reflection externally.

I have moved through a lot of judgment in the process of unwinding my own divine masculine, from myself and those around me. I have truly learned that when you are authentic and you follow your heart, nothing else really matters. You can't please everyone nor should you even try. Big change always has a messy part, and it's in these moments of darkness that you break open to the light or your own strength, self-love, and intuition.

Your core values become very clear as you strip away the beliefs that aren't truly in alignment with your soul. This process can be volatile, but in the end, the gifts that are birthed from your journey are priceless. The freedom that I have felt in being my authentic self is so magical.

Redefining my connection to the masculine within me and to those around me is a strong conduit to the deep internal work that I have done. My strong agricultural masculine roots from my father and grandfather have played a big part in who I am today. I still have variations of the old-fashioned roots of how a woman should be treated but the inner energy of an evolved goddess who has moved through the speed of light to find herself.

Wherever your journey takes you as you begin to unwind these old systems within yourself, trust in the process. Remember nothing is absolute. Energy is in constant motion. The cycle of death and rebirth is natural. You will come out on the other side of this transition with a clear lens of your own inner truth, and so it is.

EPILOGUE

This book took me three years to finish. Many times I would be hard on myself about procrastinating writing the last few chapters. I should know better than to try to rush the universal plan.

As I was completing the last few reviews of the book, I decided to go back to one of the dating apps one last time. There was one man in particular who caught my attention. He was consistent in his texting even when I wasn't. He said to me, "If you are intuitive, then you should already know that I would like to meet you for a drink."

This made me smile, and he definitely caught my attention.

I cancelled our date once, telling him that I had to finish writing this book. He was persistent and asked me again to meet him. I decided to give dating one last chance and said yes. He was willing to drive to my town to meet me. I was so done with dating and being disappointed, but something deep inside of me told me to go and meet this man.

I had even ranted to the universe, asking for a man who was like my dad, a man who was loyal, had a good heart, and was honest, open, caring, and hardworking. I felt that my communication about a relationship to the spiritual help line was disconnected when it came to men.

I put myself together one more time in hopes that the universal delivery might be somewhat accurate to my telepathic signals for a relationship. I pulled up in my car and looked to the left and saw a black sports car. I knew that this was him. My gut feeling was very strong and accurate in this moment. I sent him a text and asked him if he was here, and he replied with a "Yes."

As I stepped out of my vehicle, and he did his, I was hit with this intense energy of affirmation that this man was going to fulfill my universal request on many levels. As he walked toward me and I saw his warm smile, I was looking forward to the next hour talking with him.

I asked him what day his birthday was, and he replied with, "January 19." I sat in complete shock and replied with, "Oh wow!"

This is the same birthday as my dad's. I think that the universe heard me … just maybe.

Fast-forward, almost a year with this man, I am seeing many of the boxes ticked off that I was asking the universe for in a relationship. I feel like the relationships up until this one have helped me heal the masculine ways within myself. Through all the failed dreams, I truly began to see what I needed to heal within myself.

I was so close to calling it quits on the dating game and surrendering until this man walked up to me in the parking lot on our first date. Our relationship feels mature yet passionate. I know that this one feels like a gift for all the previous attempts at dating, and I am going to enjoy the time and see where it leads me.

Thank you to all the male relationships that have crossed my path in this lifetime. Each one of you has taught me a valuable lesson. I believe that we always fail forward, forging our wisdom into our new connections.

Dating wasn't a hobby for me. I wasn't going to settle this time. I needed to have the courage to believe that I would find that strong match that would be worth the wait through all the fishing. I could have settled into something that felt somewhat okay, but this time I truly wanted something amazing for us. I believe that life gives us what we are willing to accept. The clearer that we are in knowing what we want makes it easier for the universe to match the inner vision. I needed to move through these last few years to truly unwind the old patterns that I had instilled within. I had to blow the doors off my old perception of who I was as a woman to begin to understand what I was capable of and truly needed for myself in a partner. Watching my parents' relationship growing up was my initial caliber for my marriage. When I outgrew my marriage, I knew that it was now up to me to unwind the old-fashioned views of a relationship as I had grown deeply inside through my own spiritual work and needed a different relationship match.

I have also embraced my divine feminine and finely tuned my

intuition. My inner knowing is like a tuning fork now, which tells me when something is not going to be a vibrational match. This is a gift that has been fostered through the trials and tribulations of all my relationships. As I get older, I am not afraid to speak my truth and know exactly what I need—end of story.

I leave you with the opportunity to begin unwinding your own divine masculine. Each of us is unique and will unravel through different experiences and time. It's time to remove the armor and ignite the peace in vulnerability.

Printed in the United States
by Baker & Taylor Publisher Services